JOHN CLEVELAND
(1613–1658)

A Bibliography of his Poems

Vera Effigies
IOHANNIS CLEAVELAND
Printed for Nat: Brooke at the Angel in Cornhill

JOHN CLEVELAND
Engraving from Clievelandi Vindiciae, 1677

JOHN CLEVELAND

(1613–1658)

A Bibliography of his Poems

BY

BRIAN MORRIS

LONDON

THE BIBLIOGRAPHICAL SOCIETY

1967

BIBLIOGRAPHICAL SOCIETY PUBLICATION
FOR THE YEAR 1965
ISSUED 1967

PRINTED IN GREAT BRITAIN

PREFACE

THIS bibliography is designed to be used in conjunction with a critical edition of Cleveland's Poems which I am preparing in collaboration with Dr. Eleanor Withington of Queens College, New York. Consequently each entry is given a number or a symbol or both (D1, P10, CV, etc.); only these sigla will be used in the Introduction, apparatus criticus, and Commentary of the Edition.

I have included in this bibliography only those editions which present Cleveland's poems as a collection. Several of the poems appeared individually as broadsides, a few in commemorative volumes like *Justa Edovardo King* (1638), and most of them are reprinted in one or another of the Miscellanies of the seventeenth century. None of these appearances is recorded here.

Imperfect copies are only distinguished from the others when pages or gatherings are missing. Mutilated pages, missing frontispieces, cropped margins (which sometimes affect running-titles and pagination), and errors in binding have not been noted. In the Descriptive Bibliographies, original hyphens when appearing at the end of a line are repeated at the beginning of the following line. Printer's hyphens in the Bibliographies appear only at the ends of lines.

In the Bibliographies I have followed the methods advocated by Bowers in his *Principles of Bibliographical Description*, Princeton, 1949. Title-pages, head-titles, running-titles, and catchwords are in quasi-facsimile, but the *Contents* paragraph in each entry is not. Swash letters used as upper-case italics have been reproduced in all quasi-facsimile transcriptions. All errors in pagination have been noted, in the hope that this may help to distinguish between corrected and uncorrected states of sheets, though in the copies I have examined there appears to be very little evidence of press-correction of any kind. For the same reason I have recorded catchwords very fully. In addition to the usual practice of noting one catchword in each gathering I have recorded a number of examples of discrepancy between the catchword and the first word on the following page.

Wherever possible I have listed twelve copies of each edition or issue, and included shelfmarks in many cases where the libraries concerned have large collections of Cleveland, or the copies might, for other reasons, be difficult to find or to distinguish. The principle has been to record six copies in British libraries and six from libraries in the United States, though I have sometimes displaced one or two of these to include copies in European countries, particularly in Eire. The + sign at the end of a list of copies means that the list might easily have been extended with copies from other major libraries in Great Britain or America. I have seen the majority of the copies listed, and most of the remainder have been examined for me; in a very few cases I have had to rely on microfilms supplied by the libraries concerned.

References to Wing's *Short Title Catalogue* in each entry are occasionally complicated by the fact that I have distinguished two or more editions where there is only one entry in Wing. Wherever this has happened the Wing number is asterisked.

In compiling this bibliography I have incurred great debts of gratitude both to institutions and to individual scholars. All the libraries which appear in the lists of copies have accorded me notable courtesies and patiently answered my many questions. I acknowledge their help most gratefully. At the Oxford University Press the skill of the compositors and the vigilance of the press correctors is beyond praise, and almost beyond belief. I am also grateful, for particular kindnesses, to Dr. Eleanor Withington, Dr. Alice Walker, Mr. D. G. Neill, Mr. D. H. Merry, Mr. R. J. Roberts, Professor H. J. Davis, Professor Philip Brockbank, Mr. John Horden, Mr. Paul Morgan, and the Research Board of the University of Reading. Mr. Gordon Jones has given valuable help with the proofs. My final debt is to my wife, who has patiently shared our home with this algebra for far too long.

BRIAN MORRIS

University of York, 1965

CONTENTS

INTRODUCTION

WHEN Fuller listed Cleveland among his 'Worthies' he summed up the opinion of the age upon one of its most popular literary figures:

> *A General Artist*, *Pure Latinist*, *Exquisite Orator*, and (which was his *Master-piece*) *Eminent Poet*.[1]

The emphasis is right, for Cleveland was famous in his own day not as the Rhetoric Reader of Cambridge University but as the Royalist poet of the Civil War. Wood tells us: 'At length upon the eruption of the civil war, he was the first champion that appeared in verse for the king's cause against the presbyterians.'[2] He was primarily the poet of the political event, but his name survived the defeat and death of the King, at least for a generation or so. Printed editions of his poems appeared regularly after 1649, and as late as 1687 he is included by Winstanley in *The Lives of the most Famous English Poets*. Reaction was bound to come, and a desperate note sounds in the 'Epistle Dedicatory' to the 1677 edition, prepared by two of Cleveland's old Cambridge pupils, John Lake and Samuel Drake:

> Whilst Randolph and Cowley lie embalmed in their own native Wax, how is the Name and Memory of Cleveland equally prophaned by those that usurp, and those that blaspheme it? . . . You cannot but have beheld with like zealous Indignation, how enviously our late Mushroom-wits look up at him, because he overdroppeth them, and snarl at his brightness as Dogs at the Moon.[3]

The new generation was rejecting the old; the decisive statement had already been made by Dryden:

> . . . we cannot read a verse of Cleveland's without making a face at it, as if every word were a pill to swallow: he gives us many times a hard nut to break our teeth, without a kernel for our pains.[4]

This verdict, echoed by Johnson in the 'Life of Cowley', doomed Cleveland to more than two centuries of obscurity, and to 'clevelandize' became the mark of the inferior poet. 'Grave men', wrote Edward Phillips in 1675, 'in outward appearance have not spar'd in my

[1] Fuller, *The History of the Worthies of England*, 1662, *Leicestershire*, p. 135.

[2] Wood, *Fasti Oxonienses*, ed. Bliss, 1813–20, i. 499.

[3] *Clievelandi Vindiciae*, 1677, sig. A3v.

[4] *An Essay of Dramatic Poesy*, 1668 (*Essays of John Dryden*, ed. W. P. Ker, Oxford, 1926, i. 52).

hearing to affirm him the best of English Poets, and let them think so still, who ever please, provided it be made no Article of Faith.'[1]

In the eighteenth and nineteenth centuries Cleveland's reputation was left in the hands of local or literary historians. He is mentioned in Walker's *The Sufferings of the Clergy* (1714) but less because he was a poet than as an example of man's inhumanity to man. There is a short account of him in Granger's *A Biographical History of England* (1769), which provoked a brief article in *The Critical Review* in the same year. Both present Cleveland as a literary curiosity; they relate anecdotes about him, and virtually ignore his poems. The most detailed account of Cleveland in this period is precisely where one would expect it to be: in Nichols, *The History and Antiquities of the County of Leicester* (1795). This is a careful and well-documented piece of work which, among other things, attempts to establish the canon of Cleveland's poems, and to list the seventeenth-century printed editions. But Nichols is primarily concerned to chronicle the past, to rescue names from oblivion; his scholarly concern with Cleveland's life and works shows just how far into forgetfulness his name had slipped. The other important eighteenth-century account of Cleveland's life is to be found in an encyclopaedia, the *Biographia Britannica*, edited by Kippis, in 1784. The entry on Cleveland is written by Bishop Percy, a distant descendant of the poet, which may account for his recording zeal, for the article corrects many errors which had crept into print over the years and adds a number of new facts to the biography. But Percy, like Nichols, is concerned to record, not to evaluate, and Cleveland's reputation as a poet remained at a low ebb. It was not until an article appeared in *The Retrospective Review* (vol. xii, 1825) that the poems received critical attention again. The anonymous author quotes several of the poems in full, and speaks appreciatively of the 'lively satire' of the poet, though he prefers the 'vigorous' panegyrics on Rupert and Laud, and the non-political poems like 'Upon Phillis' and 'Fuscara'. Few seem to have shared the author's enthusiasm, and throughout the nineteenth century Cleveland continued to interest only the historians. Mayor's edition of Baker's *History of the College of St. John the Evangelist, Cambridge* (1869) adds many details to Cleveland's biography; Brown's *The Annals of Newark-upon-Trent* (1879) makes some wildly inaccurate statements about both the man and the poems; and, finally, Ebsworth contributed a long and careful account to the *Dictionary of National Biography*. By the end the of nineteenth

[1] Edward Phillips, *Theatrum Poetarum*, pp. 104–5.

century Cleveland was established as a minor curiosity in the history of English literature, and the poems themselves were all but forgotten.

The recovery of his reputation in the present century is very largely the work of two editors. *The Poems of John Cleveland*, edited by John M. Berdan in 1903, was the first edition since 1687. It represented part of the new interest in seventeenth-century poetry, and Berdan himself said: 'This edition is brought forth in the belief that Cleveland is the last and most characteristic poet of the "metaphysical school".'[1] His biography is still the standard account of Cleveland's life, and his text and notes, for all their inaccuracies, made the poems accessible to a new generation of readers. George Saintsbury's edition, in volume iii of *Minor Poets of the Caroline Period* (1921), went further to revive Cleveland's reputation. With the help of Simpson and Thorn-Drury he established a better text than Berdan's, taking into account not only the printed editions, but some of the manuscripts as well. His critical evaluation of Cleveland is judicious. He approved of the man—'He was an honest and consistent politician on his own side, and if some people think it the wrong side, others are equally positive that it was the right'[2]—and in the poems he found things to praise and things to condemn. His final verdict is superbly forensic: 'Cleveland, therefore, was not a great poet, nor even a failure of one: but he was but just a failure of a very great satirist.'[3]

It is unfortunate that Saintsbury's edition of Cleveland appeared not long after Grierson's edition of Donne, for Cleveland suffered by the comparison which ought never to have been made. He owed very little to Donne, but has all too often been thought of as simply a 'late Metaphysical', and condemned for lacking Donne's profundity.[4] Only recently has it been seen that he belongs with different contemporaries—with Cowley, Butler, Denham, and the early Dryden. Miss C. V. Wedgwood places him in the correct perspective as a political poet, a satirist fighting to defend a crumbling order, his poems compounded of savagery towards rebellion and nostalgia for an outmoded society. She describes him as 'the most sophisticated satirist writing during the war' and 'the most dexterous poet to deal in political verse'.[5] These are apt phrases, pointing the way towards a more accurate appraisal of Cleveland's achievement. Only chronologically was he the contemporary of Milton; the two poets lived in different worlds,

[1] p. 10. [2] p. 7. [3] p. 9.

[4] See, for example, Geoffrey Walton, *Metaphysical to Augustan*, London, 1955, pp. 64–66.

[5] C. V. Wedgwood, *Poetry and Politics under the Stuarts*, Cambridge, 1960, pp. 130 and 79.

and Cleveland's was the lesser. He lived, fought, and wrote in the Civil War, and it is as a war poet that he must finally be judged.

Cleveland's earliest years coincided with a period of comparative tranquillity in England.[1] He was born at Loughborough, and baptized on 20 June 1613, the year of the marriage of Princess Elizabeth to the Elector Palatine. His father, Thomas Cleveland, had been educated at St. John's College, Cambridge, and at the time of John's birth he was assistant to the Rector of Loughborough and also assistant teacher at Burton's Grammar School in the same town. In 1621 he was presented to the vicarage of Hinckley with Stoke Golding, where he remained and brought up a large family until he was sequestered by the County Committee on 14 November 1645. He appealed to the Committee for Compounding against a false accusation of delinquency on 19 February 1651, and was discharged on 27 May 1652. He was buried at Hinckley on 26 October 1652, only six years before the death of his son. Little is known about Cleveland's mother, except that she died at Hinckley in 1649. The family seems to have been godly, sober, and quiet. Thomas Cleveland was described as 'a very worthy person and of a most exemplary life',[2] and the move from Loughborough to Hinckley may well have been the most significant event in John's childhood. His schoolmaster at Hinckley was Richard Vines, a Puritan who achieved some eminence during the Civil War. Vines was a Leicestershire man, educated at Magdalene College, Cambridge, who became schoolmaster of Hinckley in or about 1624. He seems to have stayed there until at least 1640, and in 1643 he became a member of the Westminster Assembly, that heterogeneous synod, which Cleveland satirized in 'The Mixt Assembly'. He was employed by Parliament in all their treaties with the King, who seems to have had a high opinion of Vines's ability and integrity, and he was one of the Puritan divines who proffered religious services to Charles on the morning of his execution. He was made Master of Pembroke Hall, Cambridge, in 1644, and stayed there until October 1650, when he was ejected from his Mastership and became Minister at St. Lawrence, Jewry, until his death on 4 February 1656. This man, described by Fuller as 'most charitably moderate', although he seems not to have influenced Cleveland's politics, clearly instructed him efficiently in

[1] I have based my account of Cleveland's life on Berdan's, but see also S. V. Gapp, 'Notes on John Cleveland', *PMLA*, xlvi. 4 (1931), 1075–86, which corrects and supplements Berdan on some points.

[2] Berdan, p. 13.

Latin and Greek. His pupil was 'early ripe for the University, who was one'.[1]

In his fifteenth year, Cleveland was admitted as a lesser pensioner at Christ's College, Cambridge, on 4 September 1627. It is impossible to say why he went to Christ's, and not to his father's college, St. John's, but his University career is a steady record of successes. In 1629 he was chosen to deliver the Latin address of welcome to the Chancellor of the University and the French Ambassador (with his suite, which included Rubens), and while he was probably still an undergraduate he, like Milton, officiated as 'Father' of the Cambridge Revels. He proceeded B.A. in 1631, M.A. in 1635, and on 27 March 1634 he was elected to the Hebblethwaite Fellowship at St. John's. According to Wood, Cleveland was incorporated Master of Arts at Oxford in 1637, 'not that it appears so in the public register, but from the relation of a certain person who was then a master of this university'.[2] Cleveland's years at Cambridge are not remarkable for incident. Between 1635 and 1637 he was made Rhetoric Reader, and his oration on this occasion, like the various letters he wrote on behalf of the College, is characterized by elegant, extravagant expression rather than by any profundity of content. It is probably true, as Aubrey says, that within the University 'he was more taken notice of for his being an eminent disputant, then a good poet',[3] yet many of his best-known poems must have been written at this time. The Elegies on Edward King, 'Smectymnuus', 'Epitaph on the Earl of Strafford', 'To P. Rupert', and 'How the Commencement grows new' are all Cambridge poems, and probably several of his other non-political poems could be added to the list. But politics were important in the Cambridge of the 1630s, and Cleveland was deeply concerned with the issues of his time. The University was predominantly Royalist, but the town supported Parliament, and the Burgess elected for the Town of Cambridge to the Short Parliament was Oliver Cromwell himself. In the 1640 election for the Long Parliament Cromwell was returned by a narrow margin, and the remark recorded by Lake and Drake in the preface to *Clievelandi Vindiciae* shows Cleveland's view of the matter:

> When *Oliver* was in Election to be Burgess for the Town of *Cambridge*, as he engaged all his Friends and Interests to oppose it, so when it was passed, he said with much passionate Zeal, That single Vote had ruined both Church and Kingdom.[4]

[1] *Clievelandi Vindiciae*, 1677, sig. A6.

[2] Wood, op. cit., i. 498.

[3] Aubrey, *Brief Lives*, ed. Clark, 1898, i. 174–5.

[4] *Clievelandi Vindiciae*, 1677, sig. A6^{v}.

Clearly, Cambridge was a dangerous place to hold such opinions, and it is not surprising that soon after the outbreak of the Civil War Cleveland left the University and joined the King's camp at Oxford. The latest certain record of Cleveland at Cambridge is in June 1642,[1] but his poem 'Upon Sir Thomas Martin' refers to events in Cambridgeshire, and must be dated after March 1643, so he may perhaps have been there for a further nine months.

It must have been soon after his arrival at Oxford that Cleveland published *The Character of a London-Diurnall*, a prose pamphlet which aroused great hostility among the Parliamentarians. It is no more savage and unpleasant than many another pamphlet of the period, but he does seem particularly bitter about Cromwell:

> This *Cromwell* is never so valorous, as when he is making Speeches for the Association, which neverthelesse he doth somwhat ominously, with his Neck awry, holding up his Eare, as if he expected *Mahomets Pidgeon* to come, and prompt him: He should be a Bird of Prey too, by his bloody Beake: his Nose is able to try a young Eagle, whether she be lawfully begotten. . . . He is so perfect a hater of Images, that he hath defaced Gods in his owne Countenance: If he deale with Men, it is when he takes them napping in an old Monument: Then downe goes Dust and Ashes. And the stoutest Cavalier is no better. O brave *Oliver*! Times voyder, Sub-sizer to the Wormes; in whom Death, that formerly devoured our Ancestors, now chewes the Cud:[2]

The *Character* was printed in Oxford, provoked several replies, and rapidly went into its third edition.[3] It has been suggested that Cleveland was in London in February 1645, to look after the publication of the third edition,[1] but the evidence for this is far from conclusive. While at Oxford, Cleveland wrote what is probably his most famous poem, 'The Rebel Scot', and his literary activity was described by David Lloyd as 'blows that shaked triumphing Rebellion, reaching the soul of those not to be reached by Law or Power, striking each Traitor to a paleness beyond that of any Loyal Corps that bled by them'.[4] He probably found Oxford very pleasant, and it could have caused him neither distress nor surprise to learn, in February 1645, that by order of the Earl of Manchester he had been expelled from his Fellowship at St. John's.

It is not certain precisely when Cleveland left Oxford, but by 27 May 1645 he had been appointed Judge Advocate to the garrison at

[1] See Gapp.
[2] *The Character of a London-Diurnall*, 1644, sig. A4–A4v.
[3] See F. Madan, *Oxford Books*, ii. 373.
[4] David Lloyd, *Memoires*, 1668, p. 618.

Newark, under Sir Richard Willis. He seems to have been the official spokesman or letter-writer for the garrison, for when the Scottish army under Leven camped before Newark on 27 November 1645, it was Cleveland who replied to their summons to surrender. He began:

> But that it argues a greater Courage to pass the Test of a Temptation uncorrupted, than with a timorous Vertue to decline the Trial; so jealous is this Maiden Garrison of sullying her Loyalty, that she had return'd your Summons without perusal.[1]

And he ended with the phrase which several of his contemporaries quoted in encomiastic accounts of him:

> . . . I desire you to take notice, that when I received my Commission for the Government of this place, I annex'd my Life as a Label to my Trust.

This was well-phrased but futile defiance, for while Cleveland was at Newark the King's cause had been lost, and one of the poems written at this time, 'The King's Disguise', illustrates poignantly the dilemma in which Charles's supporters found themselves. On 5 May 1646, at Southwell, near Newark, the King surrendered himself to the Scottish army, who demanded the immediate surrender of the garrison. The King agreed. The story that, at the surrender, Cleveland was tried by the Scottish commander, David Lesley, and dismissed with contempt —'let the poor fellow go about his business, and sell his ballads'—may or may not be true,[2] but if it took place at all it must have happened on the 6th or 7th of May, since Lesley left Newark immediately after its surrender.

For the next nine and a half years almost nothing is known of Cleveland's life. Like so many other Royalists he probably wandered about the country depending upon his more fortunate friends. It has been suggested that he was in London between 1647 and 1649, concerning himself with the publication of various Royalist *Mercurys*.[3] This may well be so, and it was in 1647 that the first collected edition of his poems, *The Character of a London-Diurnall: With severall select Poems: By the same Author*, appeared in print. There is nothing in this edition, or any that succeeded it, to suggest that Cleveland oversaw the publication of his work, but the idea that he sought employment

1 *The Works of Mr. John Cleveland*, 1687, sig. K1.

2 It is first recorded in *The Critical Review*, vol. 27, for 1769, pp. 426–7. As Berdan says (p. 39), 'It is hard to disprove such an anecdote, but it is harder to believe it.'

3 The evidence is fully presented by Gapp.

as a journalist, pamphleteer, and poet in London after the fall of Newark is not in any way improbable. Thorn-Drury has shown, from the evidence of two poems by the Earl of Westmorland, that Cleveland was staying at Manby, in the house of Stephen Anderson, in or about 1651.[1] The first poem, 'To Cleueland before ye first interuiew at Maneby', opens with conventional extravagance, which nevertheless suggests some intimacy between the Earl and the poet:

> Though childing woemen may oft long for this
> Or that nor yeild a reason why it is
> Yet my desiers rank-wingd have hether flown
> That I to Cleiveland, He to me were known
> Whose raptures are soe elevate by art
> As y^t each science in them hath its part

Cleveland, like most other Royalists at this time, probably took good care to cover his tracks, and these are the only glimpses we have of him in a decade which saw the publication of fourteen separate editions of his poems.

On 10 November 1655 Cleveland was arrested at, or near, Norwich, and sent to imprisonment at Yarmouth. The letter of accusation against him, signed by fourteen local citizens, is preserved in the Thurloe State Papers (Bodleian MS. Rawl. A. 32, f. 331). It describes him as 'John Cleveland of Norwich', and says that he admitted coming to Norwich from London 'about a yeare since'. He accounted for his presence there by saying that he was employed by a Mr. Edward Cooke, to help him in his studies. He is accused of living in such secrecy in Cooke's house 'that none or but a few save papists and cavaleeres did know, that there was any such person resident in these parts'. Cooke's family is said to be 'of notorious disorder', and his house a resort of Papists and delinquents. Cleveland is said to live 'in a genteel garbe', though he confesses he has no estate except £20 per annum allowed by two gentlemen, and £30 per annum from Mr. Cooke. Finally, 'Mr. Cleveland is a person of great abilities, and so able to do the greater disservice'. After some three months in prison Cleveland wrote a letter to the Lord Protector asking for his release. It is a dignified plea for clemency, in which he refuses to disown his part in the War, and indeed urges it in his favour:

> The Noblest Trophy that you can erect to your Honour, is to raise the Afflicted;

[1] *A Little Ark containing Sundry Pieces of Seventeenth-Century Verse*, ed. G. Thorn-Drury, 1921, pp. 16–18.

and since you have subdued all Opposition, it now remains that you attack your self and with Acts of Mildness vanquish your Victory. . . . For the Service of his Majesty (if it be objected) I am so far from excusing it, that I am ready to alledge it in my Vindication. I cannot conceit that my Fidelity to my Prince should taint me in your Opinion, I should rather expect it should recommend me to your Favour. Had we not been Faithful to our King, we could not have given our selves to be so to your Highness; you had then trusted us *gratis*, whereas now we have our former Loyalty to vouch us.[1]

Lloyd, writing in the security of the Restoration, described the letter as being 'of so much gallant Reason, and such towring Language, as looked bigger than his Highness, shrinking before the Majesty of his Pen'.[2] Cromwell's reaction was probably quite different, but the petition seems to have been successful, although no precise date can be given for Cleveland's release. Once out of prison he disappears again. He probably continued his wanderings until, as the Preface to *Clievelandi Vindiciae* says: 'After many intermediate Stages (which contended as emulously for his aboad, as the seven Cities for *Homer's* Birth) *Grays-Inn* was his last.' Cleveland's name does not appear in any of the records of Gray's Inn, but such an omission is by no means unprecedented in the period. It is virtually certain that he was there, and as for the date, Berdan's statement 'I think we are safe in saying that he spent the fall of '57 in Gray's Inn, London' is probably as near the truth as one is likely to get.[3] Two other statements by his biographers are less certain. Wood says that he found in Gray's Inn 'a generous Maecenas', who has been identified by Dymock-Fletcher and Berdan as 'John Onebye' of Hinckley, admitted to the Inn on 14 June 1651. This is probable but not proved. Less documented, but more attractive, is Aubrey's claim 'He, and Sam. Butler, &c. of Grayes Inne, had a clubb every night'.[4] Butler certainly echoes Cleveland countless times throughout *Hudibras*, and their names were never associated at any other period of their lives. Unreliable as Aubrey is, he may well be right in this instance.

Cleveland died of an intermittent fever on Thursday morning, 29 April 1658, in his forty-fifth year. His body was carried to Hunsdon-house, and he was buried in the parish church of St. Michael Royal, on College-Hill, on 1 May. The sermon was preached by Dr. John Pearson, who was a contemporary of Cleveland's at Cambridge, and subsequently became Bishop of Chester. He had

[1] *Works*, 1687, sig. H7^{v}–H8.
[2] *Memoires*, 1668, p. 618.
[3] p. 47.
[4] *Brief Lives*, ed. cit., i. 174.

lived quietly in London since serving the King in the Civil War, and, as Fuller reports it, his sermon was characteristically prudent:

He rendred this reason why he cautiously declined all commending of the party deceased, because such praising of him would not be adequate to any expectation in that Auditory, seeing such who knew him not, would suspect it far above, whilest such who were acquainted with him, did know it much beneath his due desert.[1]

The church of St. Michael Royal, in which many Royalists were buried, was destroyed by fire in 1666.

The statement that Milton's Minor Poems were published twice between 1645 and 1700, whereas the same period saw twenty-five separate editions of Cleveland's Poems, has often been made, and for various reasons. The only thing it proves is that for one period of some fifty years Cleveland had more readers than Milton. The statement is interesting to the bibliographer, since it is not often that one finds so many editions in a comparatively short period of time, and the transmission of the text raises some problems. A general picture shows three distinct stages. First, there are the six editions and two reissues which appeared in 1647 (D1–D6), which are so closely related and interwoven that no time-sequence can be established. Secondly, there is the long series of reprints which appeared from 1651 to 1669 (P1–P17), interrupted only once by the two editions of 1658. These two editions, although they were set up from earlier printed texts, are heavily corrected and rely to some extent on an authority outside the printed editions. Finally, there is *Clievelandi Vindiciae*, 1677, where the previous printed editions are for the most part rejected, and the text is set up, as far as possible, from manuscript sources.[2]

The editions and reissues of 1647 are not easy to distinguish. Not one of them gives either the place of publication or the name of printer or publisher, and in none of them does Cleveland's name appear on the title-page. The first three editions (D1–D3) have a page-for-page correspondence, and several things suggest that they precede D4–D6, the most important being the fact that each of the editions D4–D6 has on its title-page 'Optima & novissima Editio'. It seems probable,

[1] Fuller, *Worthies*, 1662, p. 135.

[2] The relationship of the editions and the transmission of the text is fully discussed in 'The Editions of Cleveland's Poems', *The Library*, vol. xix. Since the evidence is available there, I give here only the results.

for two reasons, that D1 is the earliest edition. First, it is the best produced. It uses good type, it is attractively set out and printed, and there are comparatively few literal errors. D2, and to a lesser extent D3, give the appearance of rushed jobs, using old type, punctuating carelessly, and introducing a considerable number of misprints. Secondly, the British Museum copy of D1 is in the Thomason collection, and Thomason usually managed to get hold of the first edition of most books. This copy has the manuscript date on the title-page 'Feb: 13th, 1646' (i.e. 1646/7), so that it must have been in existence by 13 February of the year in which all six editions were published; the early date lends support to the other evidence that D1 must be the first edition. It is clear from the evidence of shared errors in pagination that D2 was printed from a copy of D1, and the textual evidence shows that D3 also derives from D1, so that the first two reprints are independent of one another, and do not form an ancestral series.

The two reissues, D1A and D2A, require separate consideration. As reference to Table 1 (p. 13) will show, both contain considerable portions of previous editions. D1A uses the same setting of type as D1 for gatherings D to G, and has its own setting for gatherings A and C (its setting of A appears again in D4 and D5, and its setting of C in D4). D1A compresses the whole of 'The Character of a London-Diurnall' into gathering A, and uses the space thus saved (B1 and part of $B2^r$) to print the poem called 'Marke Anthony' for the first time. The remainder of the gathering ($B2$–$B4^v$) is printed from the same setting of type as D2.

D2A is more complicated. Here the standing type of D2 was used to print the inner forme of gathering A (plus the single page $A4^v$), both formes of gathering B (except for $B1^v$ which is a new setting), both formes of gathering D, the outer formes of gatherings E and F, and the single page $G2^v$. The remaining formes and pages are new settings of type. D2A adds a final gathering (H) which contains the 'Marke Anthony' poem and two new poems on 'Britanicus'. The setting of 'Marke Anthony' is the one which appeared as B1–B2 in D1A; the signatures only are changed. Both the reissues were clearly called for before the type set for the first two editions had been distributed, which suggests that the first appearance of Cleveland's poems in print was a greater commercial success than had been anticipated.

The last three 1647 editions (D4–D6) form an ancestral series. D4, which uses D1A's setting of type for gatherings A to C and has its own setting for D to G, corresponds page for page with D1–D3, and the textual evidence shows that it was set up from a copy of D1. D5, on the other hand, is not a page-for-page reprint. It has the appearance of a definite and careful revision in which attention has been paid to neatness of presentation. The Harvard copy of this edition has the manuscript note on the verso of the title-page 'I bought this booke at Rotharam the 10:th of May 1647 it cost one shilling', which gives an idea of the speed of printing; five editions were published within twelve weeks. D6, a cramped and cheaply produced book, is the worst printed of all the 1647 editions. It contains the accumulated errors of D1–D5 and adds many of its own.

The table on p. 13 shows the make-up of each edition and reissue. Each letter represents a new setting of type, and the diagram shows how the reissues, in particular, make use of type already set. In describing D5 and D6 I have used π and δ to stress that these editions are not page-for-page reprints as the others are.

The next ten editions (P1–P10) form two ancestral series, P1–P4 and P5–P8, which are linked by P5's dependence upon P3. The last two editions, P9 and P10, do not depend upon their immediate predecessors.

P1–P4 all appeared in 1651, and represent a change in the presentation of Cleveland's poems. Each title-page reads 'Poems. By J. C. With Additions', and the phrase 'With Additions' covers both the ten poems which appear for the first time in 1651 and the 'Letters' and 'Character of a Country-Committee-man', which, together with the 'London-Diurnall', are placed at the end of the poems. By 1651 Cleveland had come to be regarded as primarily a poet, and only incidentally a Royalist pamphleteer. The printer of P1 is not known, but he seems to have been aware that additions were made to the collection as the editions of 1647 were published, since he uses both D1 and D5 to set up his text, and so reprints twenty-two of the twenty-three poems which appeared in D1–D6.[1]

The second ancestral series (P5–P8) consists of the editions published in 1653 and 1654. In general appearance they are very like the 1651 editions, and the only new claim made on their title-pages is that their 'Additions' were 'never before printed'. P5 is the earliest edition to give any information about its publisher. Both P5 and P6 print William Shears's ornament, a Bible with clasps, on the title-page, and in P5 the ornament contains the initials 'W. S.'. Shears had shops in

[1] The exception is 'A new Letanie for our new Lent', which was printed only in D6.

TABLE I

	Sig. A	Sig. B	Sig. C	Sig. D	Sig. E	Sig. F	Sig. G	Sig. H
D1	a	a	a	a	a	a	a	
D1A	x	B1–B2=x B2–B4^{v}=y	x	a	a	a	a	
D2	y	y	y	y	y	y	y	
D2A	(i)=y (o)=c[–A4^{v}=y]	y [–B1^{v}=c]	c	y	(i)=c (o)=y	(i)=c (o)=y	c [–G2^{v}=y]	H1–H2=x H2–H3^{v}=c
D3	m	m	m	m	m	m	m	
D4	x	B1–B2=x B2–B4^{v}=y	x	b	b	b	b	
D5	x	π	π	π	π	π	π	π
D6	δ	δ	δ	δ	δ	δ	δ	

various parts of London between 1625 and 1662, and published many of the poets of the period, including Brome, Phineas Fletcher, Thomas May, and Francis Quarles.

The last two editions of this group, P9 and P10, were not printed from their immediate predecessors. The textual evidence shows quite conclusively that P9 was printed from a copy of P7; this means simply that the 1656 edition (P9) was set up from the earlier of the two 1654 editions rather than the later. Slightly more unusual is the fact that the 1657 edition (P10) was not printed from the edition which appeared in 1656, but from the later of the 1654 editions (P8). What emerges from the study of this group is that all ten editions are wholly derivative, each being printed from one or other of its predecessors, and that the text deteriorates steadily as one edition follows another.

The two editions which appeared in 1658 are very different from the earlier ones. They are duodecimos, they have redesigned title-pages, they interpolate prose pieces into the sequence of the poems, and they add a number of poems to the collection, some genuine, some spurious. Both are very carelessly printed, and since 1658 was the year of Cleveland's death it may be that they were rushed through the press to catch a particular market. It is quite clear that P12 was printed from P11. All but five of the variants in P11 are reproduced in P12, which adds a further forty-four of its own, and in many cases both editions agee in an obvious error which has never appeared before. The copy for P11 cannot be so easily established. It is a conflated text, and does not descend from any one of the previous editions. Many of the readings which appear for the first time in P11 are too distinctive to be printing-house corrections, and they often agree with manuscript versions of the poems in the commonplace-books of the period. But the order in which the poems are printed is very like the order in P3–P10, though not identical with any one of them, and this is not likely to be the result of chance. An examination of the variants in P11 shows that different editions were used to set up different sheets. Three of the previous editions were used—P3, P6, and P9, and the resulting text seems then to have been corrected against a manuscript or manuscripts. Apart from the poems which it prints for the first time it has no textual authority, and even where its readings agree with other surviving manuscripts its evidence can be no more than supplementary. It is, in such cases, only the witness to an unknown manuscript.

The five editions which follow (P13–P17) continue the series interrupted by the editions of 1658. P13, published in 1659, is the first of the editions to bear the name of its publisher in full on the title-page. The imprint reads 'Printed for *W. Shears* at the Bible in *Covent-Garden*, and in the *New-Exchange* at the Black Beare. 1659'. It was set up from a copy of P9, and like all the other editions it corrects some of the errors of its copy-text while retaining others and introducing its own. It is, comparatively, a well-printed book, and it adds thirty-three poems to those previously published under Cleveland's name. They are contained in a section headed 'Additions', and thirty-one of them are by the virtually unknown poet R. Fletcher, the author of *Ex Otio Negotium. Or, Martial his Epigrams* which Shears had published in 1656.[1] With one exception (P15) each of the five editions was printed from its immediate predecessor, and the text of the poems shows a steady deterioration. P15, which was set up from a copy of P13, was the last edition to be published by Shears, and P14, P16, and P17 were the work of John Williams, at the sign of the Crown, or the Crown and Globe, in St. Paul's Churchyard.

From P1 (1651) to P17 (1669) seventeen separate editions in a period of eighteen years testify to the continuing popularity of Cleveland's work, and they show that even nine years after the Restoration the satires of the Civil War still had their readers. Apart from P11, which relies to some extent on manuscripts, each of the editions in this series can be shown to depend on one or another of its predecessors.

Before we examine *Clievelandi Vindiciae* one other series of publications requires mention. In 1659 there appeared the first edition of *Cleaveland Revived*, a collection of poems attributed to Cleveland which had no connexion with the series deriving from P1. The first edition (CR1) carried thirty-seven poems, and according to its title-page it included 'Poems, Orations, Epistles, And other of his Genuine Incomparable Pieces, never before publisht. With Some other Exquisite Remains of the most eminent Wits of both the Universities that were his Contemporaries'. The volume is prefaced by an epistle 'To the Discerning Reader' by E. Williamson, which is dated 'Newark, Novemb. 21. 1658'. Nothing is known of Williamson, and his preface can hardly be called a lucid document. But it does offer some information. He tells us, for example, that Cleveland wrote comparatively few poems, and he claims to have been one of the poet's personal friends:

> It was my fortune to be in Newark when it was besieged, where I saw a few manuscripts of Mr. *Cleavelands*, amongst others I have heard that he writ of the

[1] The other two poems cannot be ascribed to any author, but no one believes them to be Cleveland's.

Treaty at Uxbridge . . . the intimacie I had with Mr. *Cleaveland*, before and since these civill wars, gained most of these papers from him.

He goes on to say that he received some additional papers 'from one of M. Cleavelands neere Acquaintance', decided to publish all he had, and to intermix with them others 'such as the Reader shall find to be of such persons, as were for the most part Mr. *Cleavelands* Contemporaries'. In view of this procedure it is perhaps not surprising to find that of the thirty-seven poems in CR1 only two are genuine. The first reprint of *Cleaveland Revived* (CR2, 1660) included twenty-five new poems. These appear to have been added not by Williamson, but by the 'Stationer', who says in his brief Preface that the success of the first edition encourages him 'to use my best diligence to gain what still remained in the hands of the Authors friends'. These twenty-five poems lack even the doubtful authority of Williamson, and it is again hardly surprising that none of them is accepted as genuine. The last two editions of *Cleaveland Revived* are reprints, which add nothing to the collection.

John Lake and Samuel Drake brought out their *Clievelandi Vindiciae* in 1677 to free their old tutor's name from the indignities they felt had been heaped upon it by the *Cleaveland Revived* series. Their Preface is addressed to the Master and Fellows of St. John's College, Cambridge, and it is strongly worded:

We know you have not without passionate resentments beheld the prostitution of his name in some late Editions vended under it, wherein his Orations are murthered over and over in barbarous Latine, and a more barbarous Translation: and wherein is scarce one or other Poem of his own to commute for all the rest. At least every Curiasier of his hath a fulsom Dragooner behind him, and *Venus* is again unequally yoaked with a sooty Anvile-beater. *Clieveland* thus revived dieth another death.[1]

The edition may well have been a large one, for there are three variant title-pages; the rest of the book is printed from one setting of type, and there is no evidence of press-correction. Errors like 'Mouh' for 'Mouth' in the last line on sig. D4 persist in all the copies I have seen.

The title-pages make three claims which are not easily explained. They claim that the edition is purged from 'Innumerable Errours and Corruptions in the True Copies'. 'True Copies' probably means the earlier printed editions, and if this is so then the claim is true, since

[1] *Clievelandi Vindiciae*, 1677, sig. $A3^v$.

the errors which accumulated from D2 to P17 are not to be found in *Clievelandi Vindiciae*. The 'editors' were aware that the text of the poems had degenerated in transmission, and they tried to restore the true readings. Secondly, each title-page claims that the edition is one 'To which are added many [Additions] never Printed before'. This is something of an exaggeration, for only two small poems and a few unimportant prose pieces appear here for the first time. The third claim, that the edition is 'Published according to the Author's own Copies', is the most interesting, since it implies that the text was set up from the holograph. Unfortunately, the textual evidence does not support this claim. An examination of the variants reveals that the text of CV is not one and indivisible, and that its sources are of more than one kind. Most of the poems must have been printed from manuscript, but in several cases it can be demonstrated that the manuscript must lie at several removes from the holograph. On the other hand, three poems at least show evidence of having been set up from one of the printed editions in the P1–P17 series. In those poems where CV relies on a manuscript source its readings are sometimes inferior to those of the first printed edition (D1), but on other occasions they are manifestly better, and in one poem CV preserves several lines which are not to be found in D1. Yet everywhere between the text of CV and the holograph stand the 'editors' themselves. There is abundant evidence of editorial intervention, especially in the elucidation of Cleveland's gnarled syntax; brackets are introduced, or existing brackets are altered, and complicated grammatical structures are frequently repunctuated, sometimes creating slight shifts in the sense. The 'editors' must have considered it their duty to 'improve' Cleveland where they thought he needed it, and this must throw suspicion upon some of CV's peculiar readings. The title-page claim that the edition was published 'according to the Author's own Copies' cannot be accepted. It is perhaps significant that CV is not the first edition to make it. The second edition of *Cleaveland Revived* (1660) contains on its title-page the statement 'Now at last publisht from his Original Copies, by some of his intrusted Friends'. The claim is absurd, but it may well have been in the minds of the 'editors' of CV, especially in view of the savage attack they made on *Cleaveland Revived* in their 'Epistle Dedicatory'. The most likely hypothesis is that *Clievelandi Vindiciae* was printed from a manuscript containing for the most part good texts of a large number of poems, though these texts lay at various removes from the holograph, and that the manuscript was supplemented by the use of printed editions for those poems known to be genuine which it did not contain.[1]

CV was reprinted ten years later, in 1687, as part of *The Works of Mr. John Cleveland . . . Collected into One Volume, with the Life Of the Author.* This edition, described by Saintsbury as the 'omnium gatherum' of Cleveland's work, brings together almost everything which had previously been printed as his. It falls into three parts, distinguished by separate title-pages. The first section is the reprint of CV, with a few misprints corrected and a few new ones made. The second section reprints virtually all the poems which had appeared in the *Cleaveland Revived* series, and intersperses the 'Additions' which had first appeared in P13. It also gathers in a number of poems which had appeared in the earlier printed editions, but had been rejected by CV. The compilation is very careless, since one poem, 'To P. Rupert', appears both in the second section and the first. The third section contains only the prose piece 'The Rustick Rampant'.

The 1687 *Works* appeared again in 1699. The sheets were reissued with a fresh title-page, which emphasized the presence of 'The Rustick Rampant' at the expense of both the prose and the poems. Finally, in 1742, the sheets of the 1687 edition (now fifty-five years old) were issued again under the imprint of three publishers, Brown, Midwinter, and Clarke. The title-page describes the author as 'The Late Ingenious and Learned Mr. *John Cleveland*', and apart from the title-page there is no new material. I have found only two copies of this issue, and it seems hard to believe that in the shadow of Dr. Johnson Cleveland would have found either a large or a sympathetic public. He was a poet of his age, and that age was long past.

As no holograph of any poem by Cleveland has survived, and as none of the existing manuscript copies can be shown to pre-date the earliest printed texts, the importance of the editions in establishing the text of Cleveland's poems is paramount. From the bibliographical and textual analyses it is clear that only three editions have any textual authority: D1, the first edition, P11, because of the variants it introduces from a source outside the printed transmission, and CV, because of its manuscript sources. For the majority of poems D1 preserves a text that is much better than that of any other witness, and it is probably as close as we can get to the words Cleveland wrote. But the

[1] One surviving manuscript, now in the possession of Dr. James Osborn of Yale University, is closely related to CV. It is not the immediate source of the printed text, but it is close to that source, and is by far the most important of the Cleveland manuscripts.

long series of reprints, although textually worthless, is the evidence of Cleveland's fifty years of fame.

Table of Editions

D1	The Character of a London-Diurnall: With severall select Poems: By the same Author. 1647. The first edition.
D1A	The Character of a London-Diurnall: With severall select Poems: By the same Author. Optima & novissima Editio. 1647. The first edition, with additional material.
D2	The Character of a London-Diurnall: With severall select Poems. By the same Author. 1647. The second edition.
D2A	The Character of a London-Diurnall: With severall select Poems. By the same Author. Novissima & castigatissima Editio. 1647. The second edition, with additional material.
D3	The Character of a London Diurnall: With severall select Poems. By the same Author. 1647. The third edition.
D4	The Character of a London-Diurnall: With severall select Poems: By the same Author. Optima & novissima Editio. 1647. The fourth edition.
D5	The Character of a London-Diurnall: With severall select Poems: By the same Author. Optima & novissima Editio. 1647. The fifth edition.
D6	The Character of a London-Diurnall: With severall select Poems: By the same Author. Optima & novissima Editio. 1647. The sixth edition.
P1	Poems. By J. C. With Additions. 1651. The seventh edition.
P1A	Poems. By J. C. With Additions. 1651. The seventh edition, with additional material.
P2	Poems. By J. C. With Additions. 1651. The eighth edition.
P3	Poems. By J. C. With Additions. 1651. The ninth edition.
P4	Poems. By J. C. With Aditions. 1651. The tenth edition.
P5	Poems. By J. C. With Additions, never before Printed. William Shears. 1653. The eleventh edition.
P6	Poems. By J. C. With Additions, never before Printed. William Shears. 1653. The twelfth edition.
P7	Poems. By J. C. With Additions, never before Printed. William Shears. 1654. The thirteenth edition.
P8	Poems By J. C. With Additions, never before Printed. 1654. The fourteenth edition.

P9 Poems. By J. C. With Additions, never before Printed. William Shears. 1656. The fifteenth edition.

P10 Poems By J. C. With Additions, never before Printed. 1657. The sixteenth edition.

P11 Poems, Characters, and Letters. By J. C. With Additions Never before printed. 1658. The seventeenth edition.

P12 Poems, Characters, and Letters. By I. C. With Additions Never before printed. 1658. The eighteenth edition.

P13 Poems. By John Cleavland. With Additions, never before Printed. William Shears. 1659. The nineteenth edition.

P14 Poems. By John Cleavland. With Additions never before Printed. John Williams. 1661. The twentieth edition.

P15 Poems. By John Cleavland. With Additions, never before Printed. William Shears. 1662. The twenty-first edition.

P16 Poems. By John Cleaveland. With Additions, never before Printed. John Williams. 1665. The twenty-second edition.

P17 Poems. By John Cleaveland. With Additions, never before Printed. John Williams. 1669. The twenty-third edition.

CV Clievelandi Vindiciae; or, Clieveland's Genuine Poems, Orations, Epistles, &c. Nathaniel Brooke. 1677. The twenty-fourth edition.
Variant t.p. ... Printed for Obadiah Blagrave. 1677.
Cancel t.p. ... Printed for Robert Harford. 1677.

W The Works of Mr. John Cleveland, Obadiah Blagrave. 1687. The twenty-fifth edition.
Another Issue. ... Printed for O. B. 1699.
Another Issue. ... Printed for J. Brown, J. Midwinter, J. Clarke, 1742.

CR1 J. Cleaveland Revived: Nathaniel Brook. 1659.

CR2 J. Cleaveland Revived: Nathaniel Brooke. 1660.

CR3 J. Cleaveland Revived: Nathaniel Brook. 1662.

CR4 J. Cleaveland Revived: Nathaniel Brooks. 1668.

DESCRIPTIVE BIBLIOGRAPHIES

The Character of a London Diurnall with several select Poems

1 **D1** WING C4662*

THE | CHARACTER | OF | A London-Diurnall: | With ſeverall ſelect | POEMS: | [rule] | *By the ſame Author.* | [rule] | [two lines of six type-orns.] | [rule] | Printed in the Yeere cIↄ Iↄc XLVII.

Collation: 4°: A–F^4 G^2 [$2(+A3) signed], 26 leaves, pp. [*2*] 1–38 47 40 41 50 51 44 45 54 47–50.

HT] [beneath a row of type-orns.] *THE CHARACTER* | OF A | London--Diurnall. B2 POEMS.

RT] A2^v–B1^v *The Character of a London-Diurnall.* [no RT on B1; page-number centred in hdl. between round brackets]
B2^v–G2^v *Poems.* [same type as Set C in D2]

A1: Title (verso blank). A2: The Character of a London-Diurnall. On B1^v: FINIS. B2: Poems. On G2^v: | [rule] | *THE END.*

CW] A2 *Rabbies* [*Rabbyes*] A4^v *Species*; B4^v Till C1 The [Th'] C4^v Teares D4^v Her E4^v When F2 *Pandora*'s [*Pandora's*] F4^v *On* [no CW on B1^v]

Copies: B.M. (E. 375); Bodleian (C. 10. 2. Linc.) (4° Z. 3 (4) Art. Seld.); Oxford, Lincoln; Dr. Williams's (PP. 3. 44. 6); Harvard (*EC. 65. C5993. 645ce); Huntington; Folger; Los Angeles, Clark Library; Chicago, Newberry Library; Princeton University.

2 **D1A** WING C4663

THE | CHARACTER | OF | A London-Diurnall: | VVith ſeverall ſelect | POEMS: | [rule] | By the ſame Author. | [rule] | *Optima & noviſſima Editio.* | [rule] | Printed in the Yeere cIↄ Iↄc XLVII.

Collation: 4°: A–F^4 G^2 [$2(+A3) signed], 26 leaves, pp. [*2*] 1–12 11 13 15–38 47 40 41 50 51 44 45 54 47–50.

HT] [beneath a row of type-orns.] *THE CHARACTER* | OF A | London--Diurnall. B1 POEMS.

RT] A2^v–A4^v *The Character of a London-Diurnall.* [*Character* A4] B1^v–G2^v *Poems.* [for variants, see below]

A1: Title (verso blank). A2: The Character of a London-Diurnall. On A4^{v}: FINIS. B1: Poems. A Song of Marke Anthony, in its undivided form, runs from B1 to the top of B2; then follow the seventeen poems as in D1. On G2^{v}: | [rule] | *THE END.*

CW] A2^{v} the B1^{v} *Scold-* [*Scolding*] B4^{v} Till C1 The [Th'] C2^{v} Ime [I'me] C4^{v} Teares D4^{v} Her E4^{v} When F2 *Pandora*'s [*Pandora's*] F4^{v} *On* [no CW on A4^{v} B2]

Notes: From B1^{v} to G2^{v} two sets of running-titles are used. They can be distinguished by the form of the initial P, and are the same as sets A and C in D2 (see below). They are distributed as follows:

Set A: B1^{v}–B4^{v}
Set C: C1–G2^{v}

Copies: Oxford, Lincoln; Oxford, Christ Church (29. B. 172); Cambridge, Magdalene; Liverpool University (G. 10. 33); Folger.

3 D2 WING C4662*

THE | CHARACTER | Of | A London-Diurnall: | With ſeverall ſelect | POEMS. | [rule] | *By the ſame Author.* | [rule] | [row of five type-orns.] | [rule] | Printed in the Yeere cIↄ Iↄc xlvii.

Collation: 4°: A–F^{4} G^{2} [$2(+ACE3) signed], 26 leaves, pp. [*2*] 1–12 11 13 15–38 47 40 41 50 51 44 45 [46] 47–50.

HT] [beneath a row of type-orns.] *THE CHARACTER* | OF A | London-Diurnall. B2 POEMS.

RT] A2^{v}–B1^{v} *The Character of a London-Diurnall.* [*Charracter* A4 B1; *London* (no hyphen) B1^{v}; *Diurnall.* A3]
B2^{v}–G2^{v} *Poems.* [for variants, see below]

A1: Title (verso blank). A2: The Character of a London-Diurnall. On B1^{v}: FINIS. B2: Poems. The seventeen poems of the First Edition are reprinted in the same order. On G2^{v}: | [rule] | *THE END.*

CW] A4^{v} *Species*; B4^{v} Till C1 The [Th'] C4^{v} Teares D4^{v} Her E2^{v} Keyes. [Keyes] E4 No; [No,] E4^{v} When F2 *Pandora*'s [*Pandora's*] F3^{v} *Englands* [*England's*] F4^{v} *On* [no CW on B1^{v} D1]

Notes: From B2^{v} to G2^{v} three different sets of running-titles can be distinguished. All three are italic, but one (Set B) uses a smaller fount than the other two. The two larger sets can be distinguished by the form of the initial P. Set A = *Poems.* Set C = *Poems.* They are distributed as follows:

Set A: B2^{v}–B4^{v}
Set B: C1–C4^{v} E1–E4^{v} [*Poems* C3 C4 E1]
Set C: D1–D4^{v} F1–G2^{v} [no RT on F4^{v}]

Copies: B.M. (992. b. 43); Bodleian (Pamph. C. 80); Oxford, New College; Cambridge University Library (Dd* 3. 14^{9} E); London, Guildhall (A. 9. 4. No. 96); Dulwich College (imperfect); Huntington (114479); Chicago University; Texas University.

4 **D2A** WING C4663A

THE | CHARACTER | OF | A London-Diurnall: | With ſeverall ſelect | POEMS. | [rule] | By the ſame Author. | [rule] | *Noviſſima & caſtigatiſſima Editio.* | [rule] | [two rows of three type-orns.] | [rule] | Printed in the Yeere cIↄ Iↄc XLVII.

Collation: 4°: A–F^{4} G^{2} H^{4} [\$2(+AEH3) signed], 30 leaves, pp. [*2*] 1–13 41 15–25 6 27–38 47 40 41 50 51 44 45 [46] 47–56.

HT] [beneath a row of type-orns.] *THE CHARACTER* | OF A | London--Diurnall. B2 POEMS. H1 POEMS.

RT] A2^{v}–B1^{v} *The Character of a London-Diurnall.* [*Character* B1; *London* (no hyphen) A2^{v}; *Diurnall.* A3 A4]
B2^{v}–H3^{v} *Poems.* [for variants, see below]

A1: Title (verso blank). A2: The Character of a London-Diurnall. On B1^{v}: FINIS. B2: Poems. The seventeen poems of the First Edition are reprinted in the same order. On G2^{v}: | [rule] | *THE END.* H1: under a new HT A Song of Marke Anthony, (the same setting as in D1A). On H2: Britanicus his Blessing. On H2^{v}: Britanicus his Welcome. On H3^{v}: | [rule] | FINIS. | [rule]. H4 blank.

CW] A4^{v} *Species*; B4^{v} Till C1 The [Th'] C4^{v} Teares D4^{v} Her E2^{v} Keyes. [Keyes] E4 No; [No,] E4^{v} When F3^{v} *Englands* [*England's*] F4^{v} *On* G2 He H1^{v} *Scold-* [*Scolding*] H3 My [no CW on B1^{v} D1 G2^{v}]

Notes: From B2^{v} to H3^{v} three different sets of running-titles are used. They are the same sets as in D2 and are distributed as follows:

Set A: B2^{v}–B4^{v} H1^{v}–H3^{v}
Set B: C1–C4^{v} E1–E4^{v} [*Poems* C1 C2 E1 E2]
Set C: D1–D4^{v} F1–G2^{v} [no RT on F4^{v}]

Copies: B.M. (8122. bb. 30); Harvard (*EC. 65. C5993. 645ci); Huntington.

5 **D3** WING C4662*

THE | CHARACTER | OF | A London Diurnall: | With ſeverall ſelect | POEMS. | [rule] | *By the ſame Author.* | [rule] | [two rows of eight type-orns.] | [rule] | Printed in the Yeere cIↄ Iↄc XLVII.

Collation: 4°: A–F^{4} G^{2} [\$3 signed], 26 leaves, pp. [*2*] 1–50 [page-numbers in outer margins except p. 9, centred between round brackets].

HT] [beneath a row of type-orns.] *THE CHARACTER* | OF A | London Diurnall. B2 POEMS.

RT] A2^{v}–B1^{v} *The Character of a London-Diurnall.* [*Character* A3 B1^{v}] B2^{v}–G2^{v} *Poems.* [same type as D2 Set C]

A1: Title (verso blank). A2: The Character of a London-Diurnall. On B1^{v}: FINIS. B2: Poems. The seventeen poems of the First Edition are reprinted in the same order. On G2^{v}: | [rule] | *THE END.*

CW] A2 *Rabbies* [*Rabbyes*] A4^{v} *Species*; B4^{v} Till C1 The [Th'] C4^{v} Teares D4^{v} He [Her] E4^{v} When F2 *Pandora's* [P*andora's*] F4^{v} *On* [no CW on B1^{v}]

Copies: Cambridge University Library (Syn. 7. 64. 140^{38}); Cambridge, St. John's; London, University College; Lincoln's Inn; Harvard (*EC. 65. C5993. 645cd); Huntington (114480); Yale; Princeton University. In the Cambridge University Library copy the pagination runs [*2*] 1–22 15 24–25 18 19 28–29 22 31–50.

6 D4 WING C4664?

THE | CHARACTER | OF | A London-Diurnall: | VVith ſeverall ſelect | POEMS: | [rule] | By the ſame Author. | [rule] | *Optima & noviſſima Editio.* | [rule] | Printed in the Yeere cIↄ Iↄc xlvii.

Collation: 4°: A–F^{4} G^{2} [\$2(+A3) signed], 26 leaves, pp. [*2*] 1–12 11 13 15–27 82 29–38 47 40 41 50 51 44 45 54 47–50.

HT] [beneath a row of type-orns.] *THE CHARACTER* | OF A | London--Diurnall. B1 POEMS.

RT] A2^{v}–A4^{v} *The Character of a London-Diurnall.* [*Character* A4] B1^{v}–G2^{v} *Poems.* [for variants, see below]

A1: Title (verso blank). A2: The Character of a London-Diurnall. On A4^{v}: FINIS. B1: Poems. A Song of Marke Anthony, in its undivided form, runs from B1 to the top of B2; then follow the seventeen poems as in D1. On G2^{v}: *THE END.*

CW] A2^{v} the B1^{v} *Scold-* [*Scolding*] B2 I B4^{v} Till C1 The [Th'] C2^{v} Ime [I'me] C4^{v} Teares [Tears] D4^{v} Her E2 Is E3 *B*ut [But] E4^{v} When F1^{v} *T*hat [That] F2 *Pan-* [*Pandora's*] F3^{v} *Eng-* [*England's*] F4^{v} *On* G2 He [*He*] [no CW on A4^{v}]

Notes: From B1^{v} to G2^{v} two sets of running-titles are used. They are the same as sets A and C in D2 (see above), and are distributed as follows:

Set A: B1^{v} to B4^{v} F1–G2^{v} [P (roman) F4 G1]
Set C: C1–E4^{v} [*Poems* D3 D4]

Copies: B.M. (1476. b. 11) imperfect; Oxford, Worcester (AA. a. 6. 99); National Library of Wales; Harvard (*EC. 65. C5993. 645cf); Huntington (122454).

7 **D5** WING C4666

THE | CHARACTER | OF | A London-Diurnall: | VVith ſeverall ſelect | POEMS: | [rule] | By the ſame Author. | [rule] | *Optima & noviſſima Editio.* | [rule] | Printed in the Yeere cIↄ Iↄc XLVII.

Collation: 4°: A–G4 H2 [$2(+A3—H2) signed], 30 leaves, pp. [2] 1–54 53 54–56.

HT] [beneath a row of type-orns.] *THE CHARACTER* | OF A | London--Diurnall. B1 POEMS. G3v Additionall Poems by uncertain | AUTHORS.

RT] A2v–A4v *The Character of a London-Diurnall.* [*Character* A4]
B1v–H2v *Poems.* [*Poems* D1 D2 E1 E2] The same type as D2 Set C. [no RT on G3v]

A1: Title (verso blank). A2: The Character of a London-Diurnall. On A4v: FINIS. B1: Poems. The basic order is that of the First Edition, preceded by *Square-Cap*, *Marke Anthony*, and *The Authors Mock-Song to Marke Anthony*, with *Upon the death of M. King* interpolated after *A faire Nimph*, and with *Epitaph on Strafford*, *On the Archbishop of Canterbury*, and *On the Archbishop of York* collected at the end under 'Uncertain Authors' together with *The Scots Apostasie*. On H2v: *THE END.*

CW] A3v ced B4v The C4v *Hymen* D4 VVhile [While] D4v He E4v But [It] F4v *Pan-* [*Pandora's*] G2 *England*'s G4v *On* [no CW on A4v G3]

Copies: B.M. (G. 11490): Bodleian (Univ. Coll. [Br.] e. 2); Oxford, Lincoln (imperfect); Cambridge, Christ's; Dublin, Archbishop Marsh's Library; Harvard (*EC. 65. C5993. 645cg); Huntington; Folger; Texas University.

8 **D6** WING C4667

THE | CHARACTER | OF | A London-Diurnall: | VVith ſeverall ſelect | POEMS: | [rule] | By the ſame Author. | [rule] | *Optima & noviſſima Editio.* | [rule] | Printed in the Yeare cIↄ Iↄc XLVII.

Collation: 4°: A–F4 G2 [$3(—B3 G2) signed], 26 leaves, pp. [2] 3–9 1 11–18 [19] 20–24 23–30 33–52.

HT] [beneath a row of type-orns.] *THE CHARACTER* | OF A | London--Diurnall. A4 POEMS. F1 (section title) Additionall Poems by uncertain | AVTHORS.

RT] A2v–A3v *The Character of a London-Diurnall.* [*Diurnall.* A3]
B1–G2v *Poems.* [for variants, see below]

A1: Title (verso blank). A2: The Character of a London-Diurnall. On A3v: FINIS. A4: Poems. The order is the same as in D5 with the addition at the end of *A new Letanie for our new Lent.* On G2v: | [rule] | FINIS. | [rule] |

CW] A4^{v} Wanting B4^{v} Thus C3 Bookes, [Books,] C3^{v} Of [While] C4 *To* [Now] C4^{v} He D4^{v} *The* [*THE*] E1^{v} Refem- [Refembles] E2 *Hyper-* [*Hyperbolus*] E4^{v} Epitaphium F3^{v} A [*A*] F4^{v} From [no CW on A3^{v}]

Notes: From B1 to G2^{v} three sets of running-titles are used. They do not correspond to any set used in any previous edition, but they may be distinguished by the fact that Set Y uses a larger fount of italic than Set X, while Set Z uses italic capitals. They are distributed as follows:

Set X: B1–C4^{v} [*Poems* C4 no RT on A4^{v}]
Set Y: D1–D4^{v}
Set Z: E1–E4^{v}
Set X: F1–G2^{v} [*Poems* F3 F4]

Copies: Bodleian (Vet. A3e. 7); National Library of Scotland; Harvard (*EC. 65. C5993. 645ch); Huntington (124679); Folger; Yale; New York, Pierpont Morgan Library (W. 2. B); Texas University; Michigan University.

Poems

9 P1 WING C4687?

[within a frame of type-orns.] POEMS. | [rule] | BY | J. C. | [rule] | WITH | ADDITIONS. | [rule] | [three rows of four type-orns.] | [double rule] | Printed in the Year 1651.

Collation: 8°: ¶^{8} A–E^{8} [$4(+¶5) signed], 48 leaves, pp. [*4*] 1–12 [1] 2–5 9 7–17 8 19–56 [57] [58] 59 58 59 62 63 62 65–69 [70] 71–78.

HT] [beneath head-ornament] TO THE | STATE of LOVE, | OR, | *The Senfes Feftival.*
D6 [beneath a row of type-orns.] THE | *CHARACTER* | OF | A London--Diurnall.
E4 [beneath a row of type-orns.] The Character of a | *Country*-COMMITTEE--MAN, | With the Ear-mark of a | SEQUESTRATOR.

RT] ¶3^{v}–D4^{v} POEMS. [no RT on A1]
D6^{v}–E3 *The Character* | *of a London-Diurnall.* [*Character* D7^{v}; London--*Diurnal.* E1 E2 E3; *London-Diurnall.* D8]
E4^{v}–E7^{v} *The Character of* | *a Country-Committee-man.*

¶1 blank. ¶2: Title (verso blank). ¶3: Poems. [¶4^{v}: beneath hdl. a row of type-orns. ¶6^{v}: beneath hdl. a row of type-orns. A1: in place of RT a row of type-orns.] D5^{r-v}: blank. D6: The Character of a London-Diurnall. E3^{v}: blank. E4: The Character of a Country-Committee-man. On E7^{v}: FINIS. E8: blank.

CW] ¶5ᵛ Phy- [Phyſitians] ¶7 On [*On*] ¶7ᵛ Be- [Bequeath'd] A8ᵛ Oh B1 What- [Whatever] B8ᵛ Thus C5ᵛ Ingre- [Ingredients] C8 Epitaphi- [Epitaphium] C8ᵛ *On* D4ᵛ THE [D5 blank, CW picked up on D6] D6 Con- [Contents] D7ᵛ Whiffe- [Whiffler] D8ᵛ not E3 The [E3ᵛ blank, CW picked up on E4] E4ᵛ Com- [Commanders] [no CW on ¶8ᵛ]

Copies: Bodleian (Wood 84) imperfect; Oxford, Worcester (W. 3. 32); Cambridge, Emmanuel; Cornell University.

10 P1A WING C4684?

[within a frame of type-orns.] POEMS. | [rule] | By | J. C. | [rule] | WITH | ADDITIONS. | [rule] | [three rows of four type-orns.] | [double rule] | Printed in the Year 1651.

Collation: 8°: ¶⁸ *2 A–E⁸ [$4(+¶5) signed], 50 leaves, pp. [*4*] 1–16 [1] 2–5 9 7–17 8 19–56 [57] [58] 59 58 59 62 63 62 65–69 [70] 71–78.

HT] [beneath head-ornament] TO THE | State of Love, | OR, | *The Senſes Feſtival.*

D6 [beneath a row of type-orns.] THE | *CHARACTER* | OF | A London--Diurnall.

E4 [beneath a row of type-orns.] The Character of a | *Country*-Committee--man, | With the Ear-mark of a | Sequestrator.

RT] ¶3ᵛ–D4ᵛ POEMS. [no RT on A1]

D6ᵛ–E3 *The Character* | *of a London-Diurnall.* [*Character* D7ᵛ; London--*Diurnal.* E1 E2 E3; *London-Diurnall.* D8]

E4ᵛ–E7ᵛ *The Character of* | *a Country-Committee-man.*

¶1: blank. ¶2: Title (verso blank). ¶3: Poems. [¶4ᵛ: beneath hdl. a row of type-orns. ¶6ᵛ: beneath hdl. a row of type-orns. A1: in place of RT a row of type-orns.] D5 ʳ⁻ᵛ: blank. D6: The Character of a London-Diurnall. E3ᵛ: blank. E4: The Character of a Country-Committee-man. On E7ᵛ: FINIS. E8: blank.

CW] ¶5ᵛ Phy- [Phyſitians] ¶7 On [*On*] ¶7ᵛ Be- [Bequeath'd] *2 Wo- [Women] A8ᵛ Oh B1 What- [Whatever] B8ᵛ Thus C5ᵛ Ingre- [Ingredients] C8 Epitaphi- [Epitaphium] C8ᵛ *On* D4ᵛ THE [D5 blank, CW picked up on D6] D6 Con- [Contents] D7ᵛ Whiffe- [Whiffler] D8ᵛ not E3 The [E3ᵛ blank, CW picked up on E4] E4ᵛ Com- [Commanders] [no CW on ¶8ᵛ *2ᵛ]

Copies: Cambridge University Library (Y. 12. 36); Huntington (102347).

11 P2 WING C4685*

[within double rules] POEMS. | [rule] | *BY* | J. C. | With Additions. | [double rule] | [cross, made of four type-orns. with rom. cap. O at centre] | [double rule] | Printed in the Year, | 1651.

Collation: 8°: A–F[8] [†][8] A4 mis-signed ¶4 [$4 (B3 B4 D3 F1 F2 F3 F4 in larger fount) signed], 56 leaves, pp. [*4*] 1–81 [82] 83–91 [92] 1–2 [3] 4–14 [73 and 76 printed in inner margins. pp. 1 and 83 centred in hdl. between brackets].

HT] [beneath two rows of type-orns.] TO THE | STATE of LOVE, | OR, | *The Senſes Festival.*

F4 [beneath two rows of type-orns.] LETTERS

[†1] [beneath a row of type-orns.] THE | *CHARACTER* | OF | A London--Diurnall.

[†5] [beneath a row of type-orns.] The Character of a | *Country*-COMMITTEE--MAN, | With the Ear-mark of a | SEQUESTRATOR.

RT] A3v–F3 POEMS. [POEMS- B7 C2 D3 E3v; POEMS C6v; POEM*S.* F2]

F4v–F8 LETTERS.

[†1]v–[†4]v *The Character* | *of a London-Diurnall.* [*Character* [†1]v; London-*Diurnall.* [†2]]

[†5]v–[†7]v The Character of a | Country Committee-man. [The Character, *&c.* [†7]v] [no RT on F1v]

A1: blank. A2: Title (verso blank). A3: Pœms. [A6v: beneath hdl. a row of type-orns.] F3v blank. F4: Letters. On F8: *FINIS.* | [tail-orn.] | F8v: blank. [†1]: The Character of a London-Diurnall. [†5]: The Character of a Country--Committee-man. On [†7]v | [rule] | *FINIS.*| [rule]

CW] A5v Phy- [Phyſitians] A6 UP- [UPON] A8v Upon B3 Square- [Square] B8v Oh C4v Teh [The] C7 Angel [Angell] C8v The [THE] D8 Epitaphi- [Epitaphium] D8v *On* [On] E7 Wo- [Women] E7v FUS- [FUSCARA] E8v At F1 An [AN] F2 MA- [MARIES] F3 LET- [LETTERS on F4] [†3] hath [no CW on F8]

Copies: B.M. (11626. a. 11); Oxford, Christ Church (A. 47); Cambridge, Christ's (CC. 6. 18); Cambridge, King's (imperfect); Huntington (imperfect); Chicago, Newberry Library.

12 **P3** WING C4685*

[within a frame of type-orns.] POEMS. | [rule] | *BY* | J. C. | VVith Additions. | [double rule] | [cross, made of four type-orns. with rom. cap. O at centre] | [double rule] | Printed in the Yeare, | 1651.

Collation: 8°: A–F[8] [†][8] [$4 signed], 56 leaves, pp. [*4*] 1–81 [82] 83–91 [92] 1–14.

HT] [beneath a row of type-orns.] TO THE | STATE of LOVE. | OR, | *The Senſes Feſtivall.*

F4 [beneath a row of type-orns.] LETTERS.

[†1] [beneath a row of type-orns.] THE | *CHARACTER* | OF | A London--Diurnall:

[†5] [beneath a row of type-orns.] The Character of a | *Country*-COMMITTEE--MAN, | With the Ear-mark of a | SEQUESTRATOR.

RT] A3v–F3 POEMS.

F4v–F8 LETTERS.

[†1]v–[†4]v *The Character* | *of a London-Diurnall.* [London- [†2]; *Charctaer* [†3]v; *Character* [†4]v]

[†5]v–[†7]v The Character of a | Country Committee-man. [The Character, *&c.* [†7]v] [no RT on F1v]

A1: blank. A2: Title (verso blank). A3: Poems. [A6v: beneath hdl. a row of type-orns.] F3v: blank. F4: Letters. On F8: | [rule] | FINIS. | [rule] | F8v: blank. [†1]: The Character of a London-Diurnall. [†5]: The Character of a Country-Committee-man. On [†7]v: | [rule] | *FINIS.* | [rule] | [†8]: blank.

CW] A5v Phy- [Physitians] A6 UP- [UPON] A8v Upon B3 Square- [Square] B8v Oh C1 VVhat- [Whatever] C7 Angel [Angell] C8v The [THE] D5v *Pando-* [*Pandora's*] D8 Epitaphi- [Epitaphium] D8v *On* [On] E7 Wo- [Women] E7v FUS- [FUSCARA] E8v At F1 An [AN] F2 MA- [MARIES] F3 LET- [F3v blank, HT on F4 LETTERS.] F5 SIR [*Sir*] [†3] hath [had] [no CW on F8]

Copies: B.M. (1465. a. 36); Cambridge, St. John's; Harvard (*EC. 65. C5993. P.1651c); Huntington (102323); Cornell University.

13 P4 WING C4686

[within a frame of type-orns.] POEMS. | [rule] | *BY* | J. C. | VVith Aditions. | [double rule] | [cross, made of four type-orns. with U-shaped figure at centre] | [double rule] | Printed in the Yeare, | 1651.

Collation: 8°: A–E8 [$4(—E2) signed], 40 leaves, pp. [2] 1–8 [9] 10–15 91 17–54 55 56–77.

HT] [beneath a row of type-orns.] TO THE | STATE of LOVE. | O*R*, | *The Sences Festivall.*

D7v [beneath a row of type-orns.] LETTERS.

E2v [beneath a row of type-orns.] THE | CHARACTER | OF | A London--Diurnall.

E6 [beneath a row of type-orns.] The Character of a | *Countrey* COMMITTEE--MAN, | with the Ear-mark of a | SEQVESTRAToR.

RT] A2v–D7 POEMS. [POEMS, A8v B6 C3 C4 D3; POEMS B6v C4v]

D8–E2 LETTERS.

E2v–E5v *The Character* | *of a London-Diurnall.* [London-*Diurnall.* E4]

E6v–E8 The Character of a | Countrey Committee-man. [o E7v]

A1: Title (verso blank). A2: Poems. [On A4^{v}: beneath hdl. a row of five type-orns.] D7^{v}: Letters. On E2: FINIS. E2^{v}: The Character of a London-Diurnall. E6: The Character of a Country-Committee-man. On E8. *FINIS*.

CW] A4 VP- [UPON] A4^{v} Grea; [Great] A7^{v} *S*quare- [Spuare] A8^{v} *V*ntill [Vntill] B5 SMEC- [SMECTYMNUUS] B7 whofe [Whofe] B8^{v} The C1^{v} The [THE] C6^{v} Epi- [Epitaph] C8^{v} Were D4^{v} FUS- [FVSCARA] D5 Ino- [Innoculate] D6 Vpon [Upon] D7 LET- [LETTERS] D8 SIR [*Sir*] D8^{v} formed [no CW on E2]

Copies: B.M. (1465. a. 37); Harvard (*EC. 65. C5993. P.1651b); Huntington; Folger; Los Angeles, Clark Library; New York Public Library; Chicago University.

14 P5 WING C4688

[within double rules] POEMS. | [rule] | *BY* | J. C. | With Additions, ne- | ver before Printed. | [Shears' ornament] | [rule] | Printed in the Yeare, | 1653.

Collation: 8°: t.p. plus A–G^{8} [$4(—A1 A2) signed], 57 leaves, pp. [*6*] 1–106. Plate, 'Vera et viva Effigies Iohannis Cleeveland.', facing t.p.

HT] [beneath two rows of type-orns.] TO THE | STATE of LOVE. | OR, | *The Senfes Feftivall.*

F2 [beneath three rows of type-orns.] THE | *CHARACTER* | OF | A London-Diurnall.

F5 [beneath three rows of type-orns.] The Character of a | *Country*-COMMITTEE-MAN, | With the Ear-mark of a | SEQUESTRATOR.

F8^{v} [beneath five rows of type-orns.] A Letter to a Friend, diffwa- | ding him from his attempt to | marry a NUNN.

G4 [beneath three rows of type-orns.] LETTERS.

RT] A1^{v}–A2 The Table.

A3^{v}–F1^{v} POEMS.

F2^{v}–F4^{v} *The Character* | *of a London-Diurnall.* [*The Character, &c.* F4^{v}]

F5^{v}–F8 *The Character of a* | *Country Committee=man.* [*Character* F6^{v} F7^{v}; *Committee-man* F7; *Country Committee=man.* F8]

G1–G7^{v} LETTERS. [no RT on G4]

Plate. Title (verso blank). A1: A brief Table of the Poems and Characters. A2^{v}: blank. A3: Poems. [A6^{v}: beneath hdl. a row of type-orns.] F2: The Character of a London-Diurnall. F5: The Character of a Country Committee-man. F8^{v}: A Letter to a Friend. G4: Letters. On G7^{v}: *FINIS*. G8: blank.

CW] A2 The [on A3 TO] A5^{v} Phy- [Phyfitians] A6 Upon [UPON] A8^{v} Upon B3 Be-[Bewitches] B6 What- [Whatever] B8^{v} How C3 *Syriark?* [*Syriak?*] C7 Angel [Angell] C8^{v} What? D8^{v} Be E8^{v} Awake F1^{v} The [THE] F5^{v} a Com- [a Committee] F8^{v} that G2 is, [is] G3^{v} LET- [LETTERS] G5 *Sir*, [*Sir*]

Copies: Bodleian (Douce C. 98); Oxford, Worcester (W. 4. 5); Cambridge, St. John's; Liverpool University (J. 1. 20) imperfect; Manchester University; Plume Library; Harvard (*EC. 65. C5993. P.1653) imperfect; Huntington; Folger; Los Angeles, Clark Library; Chicago, Newberry Library; Paris, Bibliothèque Nationale. The Liverpool University copy lacks the plate and G8, but adds after G7 a half-sheet K–K4 which contains an advertisement of books sold by Nath. Brook at the Angel in Cornhill.

15 **P6** WING C4689

[within double rules] POEMS. | [rule] | *BY* | J. C. | With Additions, ne- | ver before Printed. | [ornament, book with clasps] | [rule] | Printed in the Yeare | 1653.

Collation: 8°: A–G⁸ [$4 signed], 56 leaves, pp. [*4*] 1–18 28 20–103 164 105–107. Plate, 'Vera et viva Effigies Iohannis Cleeveland.', facing t.p.

HT] [beneath two rows of type-orns.] TO THE | STATE of LOVE. | OR, | *The Senſes Festivall.*
F6ᵛ The Character of a London-Diurnall.
G1ᵛ The Character of a Country-Committee- | man, with the Ear-mark of a Sequeſtrator.
G3ᵛ A Letter to a Friend, Diſſwading him from | his attempt to marry a NUNN.
G5ᵛ [beneath two rows of type-orns.] LETTERS.

RT] A2ᵛ The Table.
A3–F6 POEMS. [b.l. stop C6 D8 F1]
F6ᵛ–G1 *The Character.* | *of a London-Diurnall.* [*Character* F8ᵛ]
G1ᵛ–G3 *The Character of a* | *Country Committee-man.* [*Character* G1ᵛ]
G3ᵛ–G8 LETTERS. [no RT on G5ᵛ]

Plate. A1: Title (verso blank). A2: A brief Table of the Poems and Characters. A3: Poems. F6ᵛ: The Character of a London-Diurnall. G1ᵛ: The Character of a Country Committee-man. G3ᵛ: A Letter to a Friend. G5ᵛ: Letters. On G8: | [rule] | *FIꓠIS.* | [rule] | G8ᵛ: blank.

CW] A2 *On* A2ᵛ TO A5ᵛ Phy- [Phyſitians] A6 Upon [UPON] A8ᵛ Upon B3 Be- [Bewiches] B6 What- [Whatever] B8ᵛ How C4 Ma [May] C8ᵛ What? [What] D8ᵛ Be E1ᵛ VVhoſe [Whoſe] E8ᵛ Awake F2ᵛ CHRO- [CHRONOSTICHON] F8ᵛ gene- [generation] G3ᵛ de- [defection] G5 LET- [LETTERS]

Copies: B.M. (G. 18851); National Library of Scotland (imperfect); Huntington (102334); Folger; Los Angeles, Clark Library; Chicago University; Boston Public Library.

16 **P7** WING C4689A

[within double rules] POEMS. | [rule] | *BY* | J. C. | VVith Additions, never | before Printed. | [rule] | [Shears' ornament, book with clasps and initials W. S.] | [rule] | Printed in the Yeare, | 1654.

Collation: 8°: A–G⁸ [$4 signed], 56 leaves, pp. [*4*] 1–90 61 92–107. Plate, 'Vera et viva Effigies Iohannis Cleeveland.', facing t.p.

HT] [beneath a row of type-orns.] TO THE | STATE of LOVE. | OR, | *The Senſes Festivall.*

F6ᵛ The Character of a London-Diurnall.

G1ᵛ *The Character of a Country Committee-man, with* | *the Ear-mark of a Sequeſtrator.*

G3ᵛ *A Letter to a Friend, Diſſwading him from his* | *attempt to marry a* NUN.

G5ᵛ [beneath a row of type-orns.] LETERS.

RT] A2ᵛ The Table.

A3–F6 *POEMS.*

F6ᵛ–G1 *The Character* | *of a London-diurnall.*

G1ᵛ–G3 *The Character of a* | *Country Committee-man.*

G3ᵛ–G8 LETTERS. [no RT on G5ᵛ]

Plate. A1: Title (verso blank). A2: A brief Table of the Poems and Characters. A3: Poems. F6ᵛ: The Character of a London-Diurnall. G1ᵛ: The Character of a Country Committee-man. G3ᵛ: A Letter to a Friend. G5ᵛ: Letters. On G8: | [rule] | *FINIS.* | [rule] | G8ᵛ: blank.

CW] A4 THE [FUSCARA] A8 Phy- [Phyſitians] A8ᵛ Upon [UPON] B1 Pair- [Paire-] B5ᵛ Be- [Bewitches] B8ᵛ What [Whatever] C8ᵛ Here D3 What? [What] D8ᵛ Next E8ᵛ But F1 AN- [An] F2 *Precious* [*Pretious*] F2ᵛ CHRO- [CHRONOSTICON] F8ᵛ gene. [generation] G5 LET- [LETERS] G6 *Sir* [*SIR*]

Copies: B.M. (1076. k. 21); Bodleian (Douce C. 418); Cambridge University Library (Syn. 8. 65. 16¹); Liverpool University (H. 54. 30); Birmingham University; Harvard (*EC. 65. C5993. P.1654b); Folger; Los Angeles, Clark Library; Chicago, Newberry Library; Cornell University. Some copies of this edition add a final gathering ¶1–8 containing *The Character of a Diurnal-Maker*, 1654. There is no mention of this item in the Table of Contents on A2 ʳ⁻ᵛ.

17 **P8** WING C4690

[within double rules] POEMS | [rule] | *BY* | J. C. | With Additions, never | before Printed. | [rule] | [rectangle of type-orns.] | [rule] | Printed in the Year, | 1654.

Collation: 8°: A–G^{8} [$4(—G4) signed], 56 leaves, pp. [*4*] 1–107. Plate, 'Vera et viva Effigies Iohannis Cleeveland.', facing t.p.

HT] [beneath a row of type-orns.] TO THE | STATE of LOVE. | OR, | *The Senſes Feſtivall.*
F6^{v} The Character of a London-Diurnall.
G1^{v} *The Character of a Country Committee-man, with* | *the Ear-mark of a Sequestrator.*
G3^{v} *A Letter to a Friend, Diſwading him from his at-* | *tempt to marry a* NUN.
G5^{v} *LETTERS.*

RT] A2^{v} The Table.
A3–F6 *POEMS.*
F6^{v}–G1 *The Character* | *of a London-diurnall.* [*The Character.* F8^{v}]
G1^{v}–G3 *The Character of a* | *Country Committee-man.*
G3^{v}–G8 LETTERS. [*The Anſwer.* G6]

Plate. A1: Title (verso blank). A2: A brief Table of the Poems and Characters. A3: Poems. F6^{v}: The Character of a London-Diurnall. G1^{v}: The Character of a Country Committee-man. G3^{v}: A Letter to a Friend. G5^{v}: Letters. On G8: | [rule] | *FINIS.* | [rule] | G8^{v}: blank.

CW] A4 FUS- [*FVSCARA*] A8 Phy- [Phyſitians] A8^{v} Upon [UPON] B1 Pair- [Paire-] B5^{v} Be- [Bewitches] B8^{v} What [Whatever] C8^{v} Here D1^{v} Angel [Angell] D8^{v} Next E5^{v} Ugli- [Uglier] E8^{v} But F1 AN- [An] F2 *Precious* [*Pretious*] F2^{v} CHRO- [CHRONOSTICON] F7 *Prerogative,* [*prerogative,*] F8^{v} gene- [generation] G2 take [Take] [no CW on G5^{v}]

Copies: Reading University (77953); St. Andrews University (PR. 3348. C7. A17); Eton College; Durham, Ushaw College; Dublin Public Library; Harvard; Huntington; Los Angeles, Clark Library; Texas University. Some copies of this edition add *The Character of a Diurnal-Maker* after G8^{v}, as in P7. Again, there is no mention of this item in the Table of Contents.

18 **P9** WING C4691

[within double rules] POEMS. | [rule] | *BY* | J. C. | VVith Additions, never | before Printed. | [rule] | [Shears' ornament] | [rule] | Printed in the Yeare, | 1656.

Collation: 8°: A–G^{8} [$4 signed], 56 leaves, pp. [*4*] 1–107. Plate, 'Vera et viva Effigies Iohannis Cleeveland.', facing t.p.

HT] TO THE | STATE of LOVE, | OR, | *The Senſes Feſtivall.*
F6^{v} The Character of a London-Diurnall.
G1^{v} *The Character of a Country Committee-man, with* | *the Ear-mark of a Sequeſtrator.*

G3v *A Letter to a Friend, Diſſwading him from his at- | tempt to marry a* NUN.
G5v LETTERS.

RT] A2v The Table.
A3–F6 *POEMS.* [*POEMS.* A4 B3 C7 D2 E6; *POEMS.* A5 B2 B6 C2 C5v D3 D7 E3 E5 F2 F5; *POEMS.* A8v B4v C6v D5v E7v F4v]
F6v–G1 *The Character | of a London-diurnall.*
G1v–G3 *The Character of a | Country Committee-man.* [*Countrey* G3]
G3v–G8 LETTERS

Plate. A1: Title (verso blank). A2: A brief Table of the Poems and Characters. A3: Poems. F6v: The Character of a London-Diurnall. G1v: The Character of a Country Committee-man. G3v: A Letter to a Friend. G5v: Letters. On G8: | [rule] | *FINIS.* | [rule] | G8v: blank.

CW] A2 The [*The*] A4 THE [FUSCARA] A8 Phy- [Phyſitians] A8v Upon [UPON] B5v Be- [Bewitches] B8v What [Whatever] C5v *Syriack?* [*Syriack?*] C8v Here D3 What? [What] D8v Next E8v But F1 AN [An] F2 *Precious* [*Pretious*] F2v CHRO- [CHRONOSTICON] F7v P*rodigy* [*Prodigy*] F8v gene- [generation]

Copies: Victoria and Albert Museum (Forster 1743); Oxford, Christ Church; Dublin, Trinity College; Harvard; Huntington (102325); Folger; Yale. Some copies of this edition add *The Character of a Diurnal-Maker* in a new edition *1–4. The Huntington copy also adds a final sheet ||1–8 containing *Cleavelands Petition To His Highnesse The Lord Protector*, *Cleavelands Letter To the Earle of Westmorland*, and the poem *A Sigh.* None is mentioned in the Table of Contents.

19 P10 WING C4692

[within a double frame of type-orns.] POEMS | [rule] | *BY* | J. C. | With Additions, never | before Printed. | [rule] | [rectangle of type-orns.] | [rule] | Printed in the Year, | 1657.

Collation: 8°: A–G8 [$4(—G4; B4 mis-signed B, G6 mis-signed L) signed], 56 leaves, pp. [4] 1–107. Plate, 'Vera et viva Effigies Iohannis Cleeveland.', facing t.p.

HT] [beneath a row of type-orns.] TO THE | STATE of LOVE. | OR, | *The Senſes Feſtivall.*
F6v The Character of a London-Diurnall.
G1v *The Character of a Country Committee-man, with | the Ear-mark of a Sequestrator.*
G3v *A Letter to a Friend, Diſſwading him from his at- | tempt to marry a* NUN.
G5v *LETTERS.*

RT] A2v The TABLE.
A3–F6 *POEMS.* [raised full-stop C8 D6 E5]
F6v–G1 *The Character | of a London-diurnall.*
G1v–G3 *The Character of a | Country Committee-man.*
G3v–G8 *LETTERS.* [*LETTERS*, G3v G8; *The Anſwer.* G6]

Plate. A1: Title (verso blank). A2: A brief Table of the Poems and Characters. A3: Poems. F6v: The Character of a London-Diurnall. G1v: The Character of a Country Committee-man. G3v: A Letter to a Friend. G5v: Letters. On G8: | [rule] | *FINIS.* | [rule] | G8v: blank.

CW] A4 FUS- [*FVSCARA*] A8 Phy- [Phyſitians] A8v Upon [UPON] B1 Pair- [Paire-] B3 Upon [Vpon] B5v Be- [Bewitches] B8v What C6 She [The] C8v Here D3 What? [What] D5 Tha [That] D8v Next E5v Ugli- [Uglier] E8v But F2v CHRO- [CHRONOSTICON] F7v P*rodigy* [P*rodigie*] F8v gene- [generation] G2 take [Take] [no CW on G5v]

Copies: B.M. (1506/295); Bodleian (Douce C. 97); Cambridge, St. John's; Cambridge, Emmanuel; Harvard (*EC. 65. C5993. P.1657); Huntington (114496); Chicago University; Cornell University; Pennsylvania University; Texas University. Bound with this edition are *The Character of a Diurnal-Maker*, which has a separate title-page dated 1657 and runs from ¶1–¶7v, and *Cleaveland's Petition to His Highnesse The Lord Protector* and *To the Earle of Westmoreland*, which occupy a final gathering A–A8.

20 **P11** Not in WING

POEMS, | CHARACTERS, | AND | LETTERS. | [rule] | *By J. C.* | [rule] | WITH | ADDITIONS | Never before printed. | [rule] | *LONDON*, | Printed in the yeere | 1658.

Collation: 12°: π^4 A–D12 F12 G2 [$5(—C3) signed], π3 signed as A5. 66 leaves, pp. [*8*] 1–65 [66] 67 [68] 69–91 26 93–124. Plate, 'Vera et viva Effigies Iohannis Cleeveland' facing t.p.

HT] A1 [beneath a row of type-orns.] TO THE | STATE of LOVE. | OR, | *The Senſes Feſtivall:*
C10v [beneath a row of type-orns.] LETTERS.
D2v [beneath a row of type-orns.] THE | *CHARACTER* | OF A | *London Diurnall.*
D7 [beneath a row of type-orns.] The Character of a | *Country*-COMMITTEE--MAN, | With the Ear-mark of a | SEQUESTRATOR.
D10v *Vpon a Scratch on a Ladies Arme.*
F4v THE | CHARACTER | OF | *A DIVRNAL-MAKER.*
F7 *A Letter to a Friend diſſwading him from his | attempt to marry a* NUN.
F11v CHRONOSTICON

RT] π3^{v}–π4 The Table.

A1^{v}–C10 *POEMS.* [*POEMS.* A1^{v} A2^{v} A5 A5^{v} A6 A6^{v} A7 A8 A11^{v} A12^{v} B1^{v} B2^{v} B5 B5^{v} B6 B6^{v} B7 B8 B11^{v} B12^{v} C1^{v} C2^{v} C5 C5^{v} C6 C6^{v} C7 C8; *POEMS*: A7^{v} A8^{v} A9 A10 B7^{v} B8^{v} B9 B10 C7^{v} C8^{v} C9 C10]

C11–D2 *LETTERS.* [*LETTERS*: C12 C12^{v}]

D3–D6^{v} *The Character* | *of a* London *Diurnall.* [*The Character, &c.* D3 D6^{v}; *Character,* D5^{v}]

D7^{v}–D10 *The Character of a* | *Country Committee-man.* [*Character* D7^{v}; *Carracter* D8^{v}; *Committee-man* (no stop) D9, D10]

D10^{v}–F4 *POEMS.* [*POEMS.* D10^{v}; *POEMS*: D11 D12; *POEMS.* F3 F4]

F7–F9^{v} LETTERS.

F11^{v}–G2^{v} *POEMS.* [*POEMS.* G1] [No RT on C9^{v} C10^{v} D2^{v} D7 F4^{v}–F6^{v} F10–F11]

π1: Plate. π2: Title (verso blank). π3: A brief Table of the Poems, Characters and Letters. π4^{v}: blank. A1: Poems. C10^{v}: Letters. D2^{v}: The Character of a London-Diurnall. D7: The Character of a Country Committee-man. D10^{v}: Poems. F4^{v}: The Character of a Diurnal-Maker. F7: Letter to a Friend. F10: Petition to the Protector. F11^{v}: Poems. On G2^{v}: *FINIS.*

CW] π3^{v} *ſnow,* [*ſnow*] A2 THE [The] A12^{v} Kiſſe B4^{v} For- [Forbeare] B6 I [It] B12^{v} He C5 Ex- [Exhauſted] C8 An [AN] C9 Ma- [MARIES] C10 LET- [LETTERS] C11^{v} SIR [*Sir*] C12^{v} The [*The*] D10 Upon [*Upon*] D12^{v} Ad [*To*] F2 But [*How*] F8 a Grid- [a Gridiron] F10 mad [made] F11^{v} CHAR. [CHARLES] F12^{v} Let [no CW on A8^{v} F11]

Copies: Cambridge, Queens' College; Cardiff Public Library; Dublin, Trinity College.

21 P12 WING C4693

POEMS, | CHARACTERS, | AND | LETTERS. | [rule] | *By I. C.* | [rule] | WITH | ADDITIONS | Never before printed. | [rule] | *LONDON,* | Printed in the year | 1658.

Collation: 12°: π^3 A–E^{12} F6 [\$5(—C4 E4) signed]. π2 mis-signed A5, C9 mis-signed C5, E7 mis-signed F3. 69 leaves, pp. [6] 1–48 94 50–73 [74] 75–132.

HT] A1 [beneath a row of type-orns.] TO THE | STATE of LOVE. | OR, | *The Senſes Feſtival.*

D2^{v} [beneath a row of type-orns.] LETTERS.

D6^{v} [beneath a row of type-orns.] THE | *CHARACTER* | OF A | *London Diurnall.*

D11 [beneath a row of type-orns.] The Character of a | *Country*-COMMITTEE--MAN, | With the Ear-mark of a | SEQUESTRATOR.

E2^{v} *Upon a Scratch on a Ladies Arm.*
E8^{v} THE | *CHARACTER* | OF A | *Diurnall Maker.*
E11 *A Letter to a Friend diſſwading him from his* | *attempt to mary a* NUN.
F3^{v} CHRONOsTICON

RT] π2^{v}–π3 The Table.
A1^{v}–D2 *POEMS.* [*POEMS.* A2^{v} A3^{v} A4 B1 B3^{v} B6^{v} B7^{v} B12 C1 C3^{v} C12; *POEMS:* A7 A11^{v} B10^{v} C6; *POEMS*: A7^{v} A8^{v} A9 A10^{v} A12^{v} B7 B8^{v} B9 B11 C5 C6^{v} C11; *POEM*S: A8; *POEMS:* A9^{v} A10 A11 B4^{v} C9^{v}; *POEM*S. B4] [no RT on D1^{v}]
D3–D6 *LETTERS.* [*LETTERS* D4; *LETTERS.* D6]
D7–D10^{v} *The Character* | *of a* London *Diurnal.* [*The Character, &c.* D7; *Character* D7^{v}; *Of a* London *Diurnall.* D10; *The Character, &c.* D10^{v}]
D11^{v}–E2 *The Character of a* | *Country Committee-man.* [*Committee-man* E2]
E2^{v}–E8 *POEMS.* [*POEMS.* E3 E4 E5^{v}; *POEMS:* E5 E7^{v}]
E8^{v}–E10^{v} No RT
E11–F1^{v} *LETTERS.*
F2–F3 No RT
F3^{v}–F6^{v} *POEMS.* [*POEM* F3^{v}; *POEMS.* F4^{v} F5]

π1: Title (verso blank). π2: A brief Table of the Poems, Characters, and Letters. π3^{v}: blank. A1: Poems. D2^{v}: Letters. D6^{v}: The Character of a London--Diurnall. D11: The Character of a Country Committee-man. E2^{v}: Poems. E8^{v}: The Character of a Diurnall Maker. E11: A Letter to a Friend. F2: Petition to the Protector. F3^{v}: Poems. On F6^{v}: *FINIS.*

CW] π2 Smectym= [Smectymnuus] A2 THE [The] A2^{v} Metalls [Metals] A5 VVe [We] A12 As [Ask] A12^{v} Kiſſe B4 Lik [Like] B4^{v} For- [Forbear] B11 Make [Makes] B12^{v} He C5 Epi- [Epitaphium] C8 Myſticall [Myſtical] C9 Ex- [Exhauſted] C10 Y'are [Y're] C12 An [AN] C12^{v} And D1 MA [MARIES] D2 Let [LETTERS] D3^{v} SIR [S*ir*] D4^{v} The [*The*] D8^{v} Thi [This] D12^{v} due E2 Upon [*Upon*] E6 How [*How*] E12 a Grid- [a Gridiron] E12^{v} ſon, F3^{v} *C*HARLES [CHARLES] F5 And [*A*nd] F5^{v} VVhich [Which] F6 *A*re [no CW on π3 A8^{v} B6 C1 C3 D2^{v} F3]

Copies: B.M. (1487. e. 3) [this copy adds *Cleavelands Letter to the Earl of Westmorland* after F6^{v}. There is no mention of this item in the Table of Contents]; Cambridge, Trinity (H. 24. 44) [imperfect, lacking π3 D2–D11 F2–F5].

22 **P13** WING C4694

[within double rules] POEMS. | [rule] | *BY* | John Cleavland. | With Additions, never before | Printed. | [Shears' device] | Printed for *W. Shears* at the Bible in *Co-* | *vent-Garden*, and in the N*ew-Exchange* at | the Black Beare. 1659.

Collation: 8°: A–O^{8} ‖^{8} *^{4} [$4 (−O3 ‖3 ‖4 *3 *4) signed], 124 leaves, pp. [*4*] 1–115 16 117–179 [180] 181–190 19 192–219 [220] 1–15 [16] [*8*]. Plate, 'Vera et viva Effigies Iohannis Cleeveland.', facing t.p.

HT] A3 TO THE | STATE of LOVE, | OR, | The Senſes Feſtivall.
F7 ADDITIONS.
M5 THE | CHARACTER | Of a London-Diurnall.
N2 *The Character of a Countrey Committee-man, with | the Ear-mark of a Sequeſtrator.*
N5^{v} *A Letter to a Friend, Diſſwading him from his at- | tempt to marry a* NUN.
N8^{v} LETTERS.
O5 THE | CHARACTER | OF | *A DIVRNAL-MAKER.*
||1 CLEAVELANDS | *PETITION* | To His | HIGHNESSE | The Lord | *PROTECTOR.*
||4 CLEAVELANDS | LETTER | To the Earle of | *WESTMORLAND.*
||7 *A Sigh.*
*1 [beneath a row of type-orns.] A BRIEF | TABLE | Of the ſeverall Poems, and Contents of | this Book.

RT] A3–M4 *POEMS.* [*POEMS* B1^{v} B2 B8^{v} C1^{v} C3^{v} E7^{v} F7^{v} G8^{v} K2^{v} L2^{v} M1^{v}; *POEMS*, B4; P*OEMS.* C8^{v} E3 G6 K7; *POEM*S. D3 D7 E7 F1 F7 G8 H2^{v} K1^{v} K5 M4]
M5^{v}–N1 *The Character | Of a London-diurnall.* [*Character* M6^{v} M8^{v}; *of a London-diurnal.* M7; *of a London-Diurnal.* M8; *of a London-diurnall.* N1]
N1^{v}–N5 *The Character of a | Countrey Committee-man.* [*Character* N4^{v}]
N5^{v}–O4^{v} LETTERS.
O5^{v}–O8 *The Character | of a Diurnal-maker.*
||1^{v}–||8 No RT, page-numbers centred.
*1^{v}–*3 The Table.

A1: Plate. A2: Title (verso blank). A3: Poems. F7: Additions. M4^{v}: blank. M5: The Character of a London-Diurnall. N2: The Character of a Country Committee-man. N5^{v}: A Letter to a Friend. N8^{v}: Letters. O5: The Character of a Diurnal-maker. On O8: *FINIS.* O8^{v}: blank. ||1: Cleveland's Petition to the Protector. ||4: Cleveland's letter to Westmorland. ||7: A Sigh. On ||8 FINIS. ||8^{v} blank. *1: A brief Table of the Poems. On *3: | [rule] | FINIS. | [rule] | *3^{v}: blank. *4: blank.

CW] A4 THE [FUSCARA] A8 Phy- [Phyſicians] A8^{v} Upon [UPON] B5^{v} Be [Bewitches] B6^{v} Then [Thin] B8^{v} What [Whatever] C8^{v} Here D3 What? [What] D8^{v} Next E5^{v} Ug- [Ugler] E8^{v} But F1 AN [An] F2 *Precious* [*Pretious*] F2^{v} CHRO- [CHRONOSTICON] F8^{v} From G7^{v} Ob- [Obſequies] G8^{v} But H2 On [*On*] H4^{v} Tor- [Tort'ring] H8^{v} Spark- [Sparkling] I4 *T*his [This] I8^{v} We K2^{v} On [*On*] K8^{v} Her L1 VVith [And] L2 Whiles [VVhiles] L7 *VITV-* [*VITVPERIVM*] L8^{v} If M2 And [*AN*] M4 The [THE (on M5)] M6 *Re-* [*Reſolved*] M8 ban- [banquet] M8^{v} But N1^{v} Fan- [Fancies] N2^{v} ſem- [ſemblance] N3 murther- [murthered] N5 beg [beggers] N8^{v} your ||5^{v} you [to] *2 *of* [no CW on F6^{v} O4^{v} O8 ||3^{v} ||6^{v} ||8]

Copies: B.M. (1076. e. 14); Bodleian (8° Linc. B. 457); Oxford, Worcester

(LR. 1. 6); Cambridge, St. John's; London, Guildhall; Cardiff Public Library; Harvard; Huntington; Yale; Baltimore, Peabody Institute; Chicago University; Paris, Bibliothèque Nationale. +

23 **P14** WING C4695

[within double rules] POEMS. | [rule] | *BY* | John Cleavland. | With Additions never before | Printed. | [John Williams' device] | *LON-DON*, | Printed for *John Williams* at the ſign | of the *Crown* in St. *Pauls-Church-* | *Yard*, 1661.

Collation: 8°: A–P⁸ [$4 (—L4 M4 P4) signed], 120 leaves, pp. [2] 1–46 31–46 63–217 [218] 219–233 [234] [4]. Plate 'Vera et viva Effigies Iohannis Cleeve-land.', facing t.p.

HT] A2 TO THE | STATE of LOVE, | OR, | The Senſes Feſtivall.
F5 ADDITIONS.
M3 THE | CHARACTER | Of a London Diurnal.
M8 *The Character of a Countrey Committee-man, with* | *the Ear-mark of a Sequeſtrator.*
N3ᵛ *A Letter to a Friend, Diſſwading him from his at-* | *tempt to marry a* NUN.
N6ᵛ LETTERS.
O3 THE | CHARACTER | OF A | *DIURNAL-MAKER.*
O7 *CLEAVELANDS* | PETITION | To His | HIGHNESSE | The Lord | PROTECTOR.
P2 CLEAVELANDS | LETTER | To the Earl of | *WESTMORLAND.*
P5 *A Sigh.*
P7 A BRIEF | TABLE | Of the ſeveral Poems, and Contents of | this Book.

RT] A2–M2ᵛ *POEMS.* [*POEM*S. A5; P*OEMS.* B3 C4 D4 E2 F4 G1 H2 I2 K2 L2; *POEMS* C2ᵛ D2ᵛ E6ᵛ F2ᵛ G5ᵛ H6ᵛ I6ᵛ K6ᵛ L6ᵛ]
M3ᵛ–M7 *The Character* | *of a London-Diurnal.* [*The Character of a* | *London--Diurnal.* M4ᵛ–M5]
M7ᵛ–N3 *The Character of a* | *Countrey-Committee-man.* [*Character* M7ᵛ; *Country* N1 N2; *Countrey* N3]
N3ᵛ–O2ᵛ LETTERS.
O3ᵛ–O6 *The Character* | *of a Diurnal-maker.* [*Character.* O3ᵛ; *Character* O5ᵛ; *Dinrnal-* O4]
O7–P6 No RT. Page-numbers centred, except p. 231.
P7ᵛ–P8ᵛ The Table.

Plate. A1: Title (verso blank). A2: Poems. F5: Additions. M3: The Character of a London-Diurnall. M8: The Character of a Country Committee-man. N3ᵛ: A Letter to a Friend. N6ᵛ: Letters. O3: The Character of a Diurnal-Maker. On O6: *FINIS.* O6ᵛ: blank. O7: Cleveland's Petition to the Protector. P2:

Letter to Westmorland. P5: A Sigh. On P6: FINIS. P6v: blank. P7: A Brief Table. On P8v: FINIS.

CW] A3 THE [FUSCARA] A7 Phy- [Phyficians] A7v Upon [UPON] A8v Run B1v *Vpon* [Upon] B4 Be [Bewitches] B5 Then [Thin] B7 What [Whatever] B8v Our C4 *Syriack?* [*Syriatk?*] C8v A D1v What? [What] D8v *Sic* E4 Ug- [Uglier] E8v Till F3 Might [Death] F5 *Pon-* [*Ponteus*] F8v That G4 O [Of] G5 Pro- [Prophaneffe] G6 Ob- [Obfequies] G8v On [*On*] H3 Tor- [Tort'ring] H7 Spark- [Sparkling] H8v Has I3 *The* [The] I7 VVe [We] I8v No K1 On [*On*] K3v *May* [May] K8v Whiles L4v Then [*Then*] L5v *VITV-* [*VITVPERIVM*] L8 *Then* [Then] L8v AN [*AN*] M2v The [THE] M4 *Re-* [*Refolved*] M6 ban- [banquet]M6v But [Bnt] M7v Fan- [Fancies] M8v fem- [femblance] N3 beg [beggers] N8v had O8v *tis*, P1 *High* [*Highnefs*] P3 ver- [verbear] [no CW on L7 O2v O6 P1v P4v P6]

Copies: B.M. (11626. b. 6); Bodleian (Antiq. f. E. $\frac{1661}{4}$); Cambridge, Emmanuel; Victoria and Albert Museum (Forster); Lambeth Palace Library; Wigan Public Library; Harvard; Huntington; Folger; Yale; Los Angeles, Clark Library; Chicago, Newberry Library.

24 P15 WING C4696

[within double rules] POEMS. | [rule] | *BY* | John Cleavland. | With Additions, never before | Printed. | [Shears' device] | *London*, Printed for *W. Shears* at the | Bible in *Bedford*-ftreet, 1662.

Collation: 8°: A–P8 *2 [$4 signed], 122 leaves, pp. [4] 1–179 [180] 181–219 [220] 221–235 [236] [4]. Plate 'Vera et viva Effigies Iohannis Cleeveland.', facing t.p.

HT] A3 [beneath a row of type-orns.] TO THE | STATE of LOVE, | OR | The Senfes Feftival.
F7 ADDITIONS.
M5 THE | CHARACTER | Of a London-Diurnall.
N2 *The Character of a Countrey Committee-man, with* | *the Ear-mark of a Sequeftrator.*
N5v *A Letter to a Friend, Diffwading him from his at-* | *tempt to marry a* NUN.
N8v LETTERS.
O5 THE | CHARACTER | OF | *A DIVRNAL*-*MAKER.*
P1 CLEAVELANDS | *PETITION* | TO | *Oliver Cromwell*, | Late PROTECTOR.
P4 CLEAVELANDS | LETTER | To the Earle of | *WESTMORLAND.*
P7 *A Sigh.*
*1 A BRIEF | TABLE | Of the feverall Poems, and Contents of | this Book.

RT] A3^v–M4 *POEMS.* [P*OEMS.* A3^v A6 A7^v B1^v B2 B4 D2 D3^v D5^v D6 F2 F4 F5^v F6 F8 G1 G3 G4^v G5 G7 H3^v H6 H7^v I3^v I6 I7^v L4^v L5 L8^v M2 M3^v; P*OEMS.* (s from larger fount) A5^v B6^v C5^v C6^v D1^v D6^v E6^v E7^v F1^v F5 F7^v G2^v G6 G8^v H1^v H3 H5^v I1^v I3 I5^v K3 K4 L2^v L4 L6^v M1^v; P*OEMS.* B3^v B6 B7^v B8 D4 D8 F3^v G6^v H1 H2 H2^v I1 I2 I2^v K1 K1^v K2 K2^v L1 L6 L7^v; P*O*EMS. B5^v; P*O*E*MS.* D7^v]

M5^v–N1 *The Character | Of a London-diurnall.* [*of a London-Diurnal.* M7; *of a* London. *Diurnal.* M8; *Countrey Committee-man.* N1]

N1^v–N5 *The Character of a | Countrey Committee-man.*

N5^v–O4^v LETTERS.

O5^v–O8 *The Character | of a Diurnal-maker.* [D*iurnal* O7 O8; *Character.* O7^v]

P1–P8 No RT.

*1^v–*2^v The Table.

A1: Plate. A2: Title (verso blank). A3: Poems. F7: Additions. M4^v: blank. M5: The Character of a London-Diurnall. N2: The Character of a Country Committee-man. N5^v: A Letter to a Friend. N8^v Letters. O5: The Character of a Diurnal-Maker. On O8: *FINIS.* O8^v: blank. P1: Cleveland's Petition to the Protector. P4: Letter to Westmorland. P7: A Sigh. On P8: *FINIS.* P8^v: blank. *1 A Brief Table. On *2^v: FINIS.

CW] A4 FU- [FUSCARA] A8 phy- [Phyſicians] A8^v Upon [UPON] B1 Pair- [Pair-royall] B5^v Be- [Bewitches] B8^v What [Whatever] C8^v Here D3 What? [What] D8^v Next E2^v *T*here [There] E5^v Ug- [Ugler] E7 *T*he [The] E8^v But [*B*ut] F1 AN [An] F2 *Precions* [P*retious*] F2^v CHRO- [CHRONO-STICON] F8^v *F*rom [From] G7^v Ob- [Obſequies] G8^v But H1 Like [*L*ike] H2 On [*On*] H4^v Tor- [Tort'ring] H7^v *E*arth [Earth] H8^v *S*park- [Sparkling] I6 Smiling [*S*miling] I8^v We K1^v To [*T*o] K2^v On [*On*] K5 May- [May] K6 *T*he [The] K8^v Her L1 With [And] L7 *VITV-* [*VITVPERIVM*] L8^v If M4 *T*he [THE (on M5)] M6 *Re-* [*Reſolved*] M8 ban- [banquet] M8^v But N1^v Fan- [Fancies] N2^v ſem- [ſemblance] N3 murther- [murthered] N4^v noe [one] N5 beg [beggers] N8^v your P3 up *1 *The* [no CW on D7 F6^v O4^v O8 P3^v P6^v P8]

Copies: B.M. (11626. a. 14); Bodleian (Vet. A3f. 1177); Oxford, Exeter; Cambridge University Library (Syn. 8. 66. 43^1); Victoria & Albert Museum (Forster); National Library of Scotland; Huntington; Yale; New York Public Library (Berg); Princeton University; Texas University; Baltimore, Peabody Institute. +

25 **P16** WING C4697

[within double rules] POEMS. | [rule] | BY | John Cleaveland. | With Additions, never before | Printed. | [double rule] | [Williams' Crown and Globe device] | [double rule] | *London*, Printed by *S. G.* for

John Williams at | the *Crown* & *Globe* in St. *Pauls* Church-yard, 1665.

Collation: 8°: A–P^{8} [$4 signed], 120 leaves, pp. [*4*] 1–20 12 22–121 120 121 124–142 147 144–146 143 148–149 151 150 152–178 [179] 180–214 115 216–232 [*4*].

HT] A3 [beneath a row of type-orns.] TO THE | STATE of LOVE, | OR | The Senſes Feſtival.
F7 ADDITIONS
M4^{v} THE | CHARACTER | Of a London-Diurnal.
N1^{v} *The Character of a Country Committee-man, with* | *the Ear mark of a Sequeſtrator.*
N5 *A Letter to a Friend diſſwading him from his* | *attemptt to marry a* NUN.
N8 LETTERS.
O4^{v} THE | CHARACTER | OF | *A DIVRNAL-MAKER.*
O8 CLEAVELANDS | *PETTITION* | TO | *Oliver Cromwell,* | Late PROTECTOR.
P3 CLEAVELANDS LETTER | To the Earl of | *WESTMORLAND.*
P5^{v} *A Sigh.*
P7 A BRIEF | TABLE | Of the ſeverall Poems and contents | of this Book.

RT] A3^{v}–M4 *POEMS*. [*POEMS*, G1]
M5–N1 *A Character* | *of a London Diurnal.*
N1^{v}–N4^{v} *The Character of a* | *Country Committee-man.* [*Countrey* N2; *The Character of a, &c.* N4^{v}]
N5–O4 LETTERS. [LETTRS. O2^{v}]
O5–O7^{v} *The Character* | *of a Diurnal-maker.* [*Diurnal maker.* O7; *The Character of a, &c.* O7^{v}]
O8–P7 No RT.
P7^{v}–P8^{v} The Table.

A1: Plate. A2: Title (verso blank). A3: Poems. F7: Additions. M4^{v}: The Character of a London-Diurnall. N1^{v}: The Character of a Country Committee--man. N5: A Letter to a Friend. N8: Letters. O4^{v}: The Character of a Diurnal--Maker. On O7^{v}: *FINIS*. O8: Cleveland's Petition to the Protector. P3: Letter to Westmorland. P5^{v}: A Sigh. On P6^{v}: *FINIS*. P7: A Brief Table. On P8^{v}: FINIS.

CW] A4 FU- [FUSCARA] A8 Phy- [Phyſicians] A8^{v} Upon [UPON] B5^{v} Be- [Bewitches] B8^{v} What C5 'Gainſt [Gainſt] C5^{v} *Syriak*; [*Syriack?*] C6 *T*he [The] C8 be [Be] C8^{v} Here D8^{v} Next E5^{v} Ug- [Uglier] E8^{v} But F1 And [An] F6^{v} AD- [ADDITIONS] F8^{v} From G7 P*i*ae [Piae] G8^{v} But H2 On [*On*] H3 *T*he [The] H7 Nor [Not] H8^{v} Spark- [Sparkling] I4 *T*his [This] I8^{v} We K1^{v} *T*o [To] K2^{v} On [*On*] K5 May- [May] K8^{v} Her L7^{v} For [Fot] L8^{v} If M4 The [THE] M5^{v} *Re-* [*Reſolved*] M8^{v} that N1 Fan= [Fancies] N6 ſtomes [ſtones] N8^{v} gift O5 writer, [Writer,] O8^{v} that P2 eſta- [eſtablish] P2^{v} Cleave- [CLEAVELANDS] [no CW on O7^{v} P6^{v}]

Copies: B.M. (11626. b. 11); Cambridge, St. John's; Cambridge, Christ's; Durham University; Harvard (*EC. 65. C5993. P.1665); Huntington; Folger; Los Angeles, Clark Library; Michigan University.

26 **P17** WING C4698

POEMS. | [rule] | BY | John Cleaveland. | With Additions, never before | Printed. | [double rule] | [Williams' crown device] | [double rule] | *LONDON*,| Printed by *J.R.* for *John Williams*, 1669.

Collation: 8°: A–P⁸ [$4 (—P4) signed], 120 leaves, pp. [*4*] 1–2 [3] [4] 5–8 [9] 10–26 54 28–118 116 120 121 120 121 124–230 [*6*] Plate 'Vera et viva Effigies Johannis Cleeveland', facing t.p.

HT] A3 [beneath a row of type-orns.] TO THE | STATE of LOVE, | OR | *The Senſes Feſtival.*
F7 ADDITIONS
M4ᵛ THE | CHARACTER | Of a London Diurnal.
N1ᵛ *The Character of a Countrey Committee-man*, | *with the Ear mark of a Sequeſtrator.*
N5 *A Letter to a Friend diſſwading him from his* | *attempt to marry a* NUN.
N8 LETTERS.
O4ᵛ THE | CHARACTER | OF | *A DIVRNAL-MAKER.*
O8 CLEAVELANDS | *PETITION* | TO | *Oliver Cromwell*, | Late PROTECTOR.
P2 CLEAVELANDS | LETTER | To the Earl of | *WESTMORLAND.*
P4ᵛ *A Sigh.*
P6 A BRIEF | TABLE | Of the ſeverall Poems and contents | of this Book.

RT] A3ᵛ–M4 *POEMS*. [*POEMS*. A7ᵛ A8ᵛ L1ᵛ; P*OEMS*. B2 B5 E5ᵛ E6ᵛ E7 G2 G8ᵛ H1 I8ᵛ K2 K3ᵛ K7ᵛ; *POEMS* B5ᵛ B6 D2 F3ᵛ F6 M4; *POEM*S. E1 G1ᵛ G2ᵛ G4ᵛ H1ᵛ I2 K4; P*OEM*S E4; PO*EM*S. E4ᵛ E5 E8ᵛ I4ᵛ I5 K1 K5 K5ᵛ K7 K8 K8ᵛ; *POEMS*: E8 I3; *POEMS*. L1 L5 L6 L8 M2 M3ᵛ; *POEMS* L3ᵛ; *POEM*S. C3 D8; *BOEMS*. I8]
M5–N1 *A Character* | *of a London Diurnal*. [*Character*. M5ᵛ; *Character* M7ᵛ]
N1ᵛ–N4ᵛ *The Character of a* | *Countrey Committee-man*. [*Countrey* N4; *committee-man*. N2; *The Character of a, &c.* N4ᵛ]
N5–O4 LETTERS.
O5–O7ᵛ *The Character* | *of a Diurnal-maker*. [*Character* O6ᵛ; *Diurnal maker*. O7; *The Character of a, &c.* O7ᵛ]
O8–P6 No RT.
P6ᵛ–P7ᵛ The Table.

A1: Plate. A2: Title (verso blank). A3: Poems. F7: Additions. M4^v: The Character of a London-Diurnall. N1^v: The Character of a Country Committee--man. N5: A Letter to a Friend. N8: Letters. O4^v: The Character of a Diurnal Maker. On O7^v: *FINIS*. O8: Cleveland's Petition to the Protector. P4^v: A Sigh. On P5^v: *FINIS*. P6: A Brief Table. On P7^v: *FINIS*. P8 blank.

CW] A4 FU- [FUSCARA] A8 Phy- [Phyſicians] A8^v Upon [UPON] B5^v Be- [Bewitches] B8^v What C5 'Gainſt [Gainſt] C5^v *Syriack;* [*Syriack?*] C8^v Here D8^v Next E5^v Vg- [Uglier] E8 Unleſſe [Unleſs] E8^v But F1 And [An] F2 *Praeci-* [*Precious*] F3 Strange. [Strange] G1 *F*rom [From] G2^v VVhen [When] G3 VVas [Was] G7^v Ob. [Obſequies.] G8^v But H1 *L*ike [Like] H2 On [O*n*] H7 Nor [Not] H8^v Spark- [Sparkling] I3^v *T*he [The] I8^v We [VVe] K2^v On [*On*] K8^v Her L1^v When, [When] L2^v The [*The*] L8^v If M4 The [THE] M8^v that N1 Fan- [Fancies] N6 ſtomes [ſtones] N8^v gift O5 writer, [Writer,] O8^v Methinks P1^v Cleave- [CLEAVELANDS] P3 yet [Yet] P3^v epithet [epithets] [no CW on F8^v O7^v P5^v]

Copies: B.M. (11630. aa. 1) imperfect; Bodleian (Radcliffe f. 84); Oxford, Christ Church; Oxford, Worcester (LR. 1. 5); Liverpool University; Harvard (*EC. 65. C5993. P1669); Huntington; Yale; Chicago University; Texas University; Michigan University; Berlin, Deutsche Staatsbibliothek. + Some copies of this edition print the page-number on p. 58 in the inner margin.

Clievelandi Vindiciae

27 **CV** WING C4669–71

[within double rules] *Clievelandi Vindiciae*; | OR, | CLIEVELAND'S | Genuine POEMS, | Orations, Epiſtles, *&c.* | Purged from the many | Falſe & Spurious Ones | Which had uſurped his Name, and | from innumerable Errours and | Corruptions in the True. | [rule] | To which are added many never | Printed before. | [rule] | Publiſhed according to the Author's own Copies. | [rule] | *LONDON*, | Printed for *Nath. Brooke*, at the *Angel* in *Corne-* | *Hill* near the *Royal Exchange*, 1677.

Collation: 8°: A^8 a^4 B–Q^8 [$4 (—a3 a4) signed], 132 leaves, pp. [*24*] 1–239 [240]. Plate, 'Vera Effigies IOHANNIS CLEAVELAND' facing t.p.

HT] A3 [beneath a double rule] TO THE | Right Worſhipful | And Reverend | FRANCIS TURNER *D.D.*
A6 [beneath a double rule] *A ſhort Account of the Author's* | *Life.*
A8^v CLIEVELANDI Manibus, | Parentalia.
B1 [beneath two rows of type-orns.] CLEVELAND's Poems | Digeſted in Order. | SECT. I. | Containing | LOVE-POEMS.

C8 [beneath a double rule] SECT. II. | Containing Poems which re- | late to State-Affairs.

F5^{v} [beneath a double rule] SECT. III. | Containing Miscellanies.

RT] A3^{v}–A5^{v} The Epiftle | Dedicatory. [The Epiftle, *&c.* A5^{v}]

A6–Q8 No RT. From B1 page numbers centred in hdl. between square brackets.

A1: Plate. A2: Title (verso blank). A3: Epistle Dedicatory. A6: A short account of the Author's Life. A8^{v}: Clievelandi Manibus Parentalia. B1: Section One, Love Poems. C8: Section Two, Poems which relate to State-Affairs. F5^{v}: Section Three, Containing Miscellanies. [This section contains the following items: F5^{v}–G6^{v}: Poems. G7–H3: The Character of a Country Committee-man. H3–H6^{v}: The Character of a Diurnal Maker. H6^{v}–I4: The Character of a London-Diurnall. I4–K1: Four Letters (the Newark correspondence). K1^{v}- K7^{v}: An Answer to a Pamphlet written against the Lord Digby's Speech. K7^{v}–L1^{v}: Cleveland's Petition to the Protector. L1^{v}–L3: Two letters on behalf of St. John's College. L3–L5: Letter to Westmorland. L5–L8^{v}: A Letter to a Friend. M1–M4^{v}: The Piece of a Common Place upon *Romans* the 4th. Last Verse. M5–M6^{v}: The Answer to the Newark-Summons. M7–N6^{v}: Six Latin Orations. N7–N8^{v}: Actus primi Scena secunda. O1–P4^{v}: Five Latin Orations. P5–Q7: Eleven letters on behalf of St. John's College. Q7^{v}–Q8: Vinum est Poetarum Equus. On Q8: | [rule] | FINIS. | [rule] | Q8^{v}: blank.]

CW] A7 Thence- [Thenceforth] A8 Clievelandi [Clievelandi] a2 *Both* a4^{v} *Clieveland*'s [Cleveland's] B5 To [To morrow] B8^{v} *Upon* C8^{v} Quits D7^{v} *Aut* [*The*] D8 Or [*Aut*] D8^{v} *Pene* [Or] E1 The [*Pene*] E1^{v} *Nec* [The] E2 And [*Nec*] E2^{v} *Seri* [And] E3 Rebels [*Seri*] E3^{v} Americanus [Rebels] E4 The [Americanus] E8^{v} But F8^{v} 'Tis G1^{v} Epita- [Epitaphium] G8^{v} *componitur*; H3^{v} Ends. [Ends,] H8^{v} lour I8^{v} though K3 *There-* [*Therefore*] K8^{v} your L4 Pane- [Panegyrick] L6^{v} other [ther] L8 ftart, [Start,] L8^{v} The M3 *deftroy* [*destroy*] M6 rermine. [termine.] M8^{v} *ufque* N8^{v} Oratio O8^{v} *cumque* P8^{v} Epiftola Q3^{v} Edvardo [*Edvardo*] [no CW on E4^{v} M4^{v}]

Copies: Bodleian (Douce CC. 150); Oxford, Magdalen; Cambridge, St. John's; London University; Liverpool University (J. 3. 32); Manchester University; Harvard (*EC. 65. C5993. B677c); Huntington; Yale (imperfect); Folger; Chicago, Newberry Library; Princeton University. +

Notes: There were probably three issues of this edition, all dated 1677. They were printed from one setting of type, and are identical apart from their title-pages. The title-pages of the other two issues are as follows:

[within double rules] *Clievelandi Vindiciae*; | OR, | CLIEVELAND'S | Genuine Poems, | Orations, Epiftles, *&c.* | Purged from the many | Falfe & Spurious Ones | Which had ufurped his Name, and | from innumerable Errours and | Corruptions in the true Copies. | [rule] | To which are added many Additions | never Printed before: With an Ac- | count of the Author's Life. | [rule] | Publiſhed according to the Author's own Copies. | [rule] | *LONDON*, | Printed for *Obadiah Blagrave*, at the Sign of the | *Bear* in St. *Paul*'s Church Yard, near the Little North | Door, 1677.

Copies: B.M. (G. 18853); Oxford, Christ Church; Cambridge, St. John's; Liverpool University (H. 47.13); National Library of Scotland; Birmingham University; Harvard (*EC. 65. C5993. B677ca); Huntington; New York Public Library; Chicago, Newberry Library; Texas University; Princeton University. +

[within double rules] *CLIEVELANDI VINDICIÆ*: | OR, | CLIEVELAND's | Genuine Poems, | Orations, Epiſtles, *&c.* | PURGED FROM | *The many Falſe and Spurious Ones* | *which had uſurped his Name*, | And from innumerable Errours and | Corruptions in the True Copies. | [rule] | *To which are added many never Printed* | *before, with an account of the Author's Life.* | [rule] | Publiſhed according to the Author's | own Copies. | [double rule] | *LONDON*, | Printed for *Robert Harford*, at the *Angel* in | *Cornhill* near the *Royal-Exchange*, 1677.

Copies: London, Guildhall; Liverpool University (Knowsley 105); Birmingham University; St. Andrews University; Durham University; Dublin, Archbishop Marsh's Library; Harvard (*EC. 65. C5993. B677caa); Huntington; Yale; Los Angeles, Clark Library; Michigan University; Cornell University. +

This title-page is a cancel in all copies examined.

The Works of Mr. John Cleveland

28 **W** WING C4654–5

[within double rules] THE | WORKS | OF | Mr. John Cleveland, | Containing his | *Poems, Orations, Epiſtles,* | Collected into | **One Volume,** | With the | LIFE | Of the | AUTHOR. | [rule] | *LONDON*, | Printed by *R. Holt*, for *Obadiah Blagrave*, | at the *Bear* and *Star*, over againſt the little | North Door in St. *Paul*'s Church- | Yard. 1687.

Second t.p. (N3) [within double rules] John Cleaveland's | **Revived** | POEMS, | Orations, | EPISTLES, | And other of his Genuine | INCOMPARABLE PIECES | Now at laſt Publiſhed from his | Original Copies by ſome of his | intruſted Friends. | [rule] | *Non norunt haec monumenta mori.* | [rule] | *LONDON*, | Printed by *R. Holt*, for *Obadiah Blagrave*, | at the *Bear* in St. *Paul*'s Church-yard. 1687.

Third t.p. (Cc1) [within double rules] THE | Ruſtick Rampant, | OR | RURAL ANARCHY | AFFRONTING | **Monarchy:** | IN THE | INSURRECTION | OF | WAT TYLER. | [rule] | By *J.C.* | [rule] |

Claudian. | *Aſperius nihil eſt humili cum ſurgit in altum.* | [rule] | *LONDON,* | Printed by *R. Holt,* for *Obadiah Blagrave,* | at the *Bear* in St. *Paul's* Church-yard. 1687.

Collation: 8°: A⁸ a⁴ B–Ll⁸ [$4 (—a3 a4 N2 N3 Cc1) signed]. 276 leaves, pp. [*24*] 1–109 111 110 112–144 143 144–177 [178] [179] [180] 181–182 179 184–185 182 183 188 189 186 193–235 136 237–384 [385] [386] 387–514 [*14*]. Plate, 'Vera Effigies IOHANNIS CLEAVELAND' facing t.p.

HT] A3 [beneath two rules] TO THE | Right Worſhipful | And Reverend | FRANCIS TURNER *D.D.*

A6 [beneath two rules] *A ſhort Account of the Author's* | *Life.*

A8ᵛ CLEVELANDI Manibus, | Parentalia.

B1 [beneath two rules] CLEVELAND'S | POEMS. | Digeſted in Order. | [rule] | SECT. I. | *Containing Love-Poems.* | [rule] |

C4ᵛ [beneath two rules] SECT. II. | Containing POEMS which re- | late to STATE-AFFAIRS. | [rule] |

E5ᵛ [beneath two rules] SECT. III. | Containing MISCELLANIES. | [rule] |

N4 [beneath two rules] To the HECTORS, upon | the unfortunate death of H. | COMPTON.

O4ᵛ ADDITIONS.

Cc2 [beneath two rules] *John* of Lydgate, *Lib.* 4.

Cc3 [beneath two rules] To the Reader.

Cc7 [beneath two rules] THE | **Rustick Rampant,** | OR | RURAL ANARCHY.

Ll2 [beneath two rules] A | TABLE | TO | Mr. *John Cleveland's* | WORKS. | [rule] |

Ll7 *Books Printed for and ſold by* Obadiah Blagrave *at the* | Black Bear *and* Star *in St.* Pauls Church-yard, *o-* | *ver againſt the little North-Door.*

RT] A3ᵛ–A5ᵛ The Epiſtle | Dedicatory. [Dedicatory A5; The Epiſtle, *&c.* A5ᵛ]

A6ᵛ–A8 Cleveland's *Life.*

a1–Ll1ᵛ No RT. [from B1 page-numbers centred in hdl. between round brackets]

Ll2ᵛ–Ll6ᵛ The Table.

Ll7ᵛ–Ll8ᵛ *Books ſold by* Obadiah Blagrave.

A1: Plate. A2: Title (verso blank). A3: Epistle Dedicatory. A6: Life of Cleveland. A8ᵛ: Clevelandi Manibus Parentalia. B1: Section I. Love Poems. C4ᵛ: Section II. Poems which relate to State-Affairs. E5ᵛ: Section III. Miscellanies. [This section contains the following items: E5ᵛ–F4: Poems. F4ᵛ–F7ᵛ: The Character of a Country Committee-man. F7ᵛ–G2: The Character of a Diurnal Maker. G2–G6ᵛ: The Character of a London-Diurnall. G6ᵛ–H2: Four letters (the Newark correspondence). H2ᵛ–H6ᵛ: An Answer to a Pamphlet written against the Lord Digby's speech. H7–H8v: Cleveland's Petition to the Protector. H8v–I3: Three Letters. I3–I6: A Letter to a Friend. I6–K1: The Piece of a Common-Place upon Romans the 4th. Last Verse. K1–K2: The Answer to the Newark-Summons. K2v–K7v: Six Latin Orations. K8–L1: Actus Primi scena Secunda. L1v–M1v: Five Latin Orations. M2–N1v: Eleven Letters on behalf of St. John's College. N2: Vinum est Poetarum Equus. On N2: FINIS. N2v: blank.] N3: Second Title (verso blank). N4: Poems. O4v: Additions. On Bb8v: *FINIS* Cc1: Third Title (verso blank). Cc2: John of Lydgate, Lib. 4. Cc3: To the Reader. Cc7: The Rustick Rampant. On Ll1v: *FINIS*. Ll2: A Table to Mr. John Cleveland's Works. Ll7: Books Printed for Obadiah Blagrave. On Ll8v: FINIS.

CW] A8 Clevelandi. [CLEVELANDI] a4v *Cleveland's* [CLEVELAND'S] B7v *The* [*To*] C1v Or [Oh] D8v Come F8v Skip- G8v *Mr.* H1 Languages [Language] I8v Thieves, K3v *tiæ.* [*tiæ.*] L8 *dentia* [*dentiâ*] M8v Ad N1 *Ubi* [U*Bi*] N7 An [*An*] O8v No P8v Thy Q8v Whiles R8v He S8v Whom T8v Hence V8 On [*On*] X8v There's Y2 'Tis [''Tis] Y7v A[*A*] Z8v Gems Aa8v 12. 'Tis Cc6v The [THE] Dd3 gvie [give] Ee8v Eaſt-Angles, Ff8v whether Gg8v and Hh8v he [He] Ii4v *places* [*Places*] Kk8v are Ll2 A [O*n*] Ll2v A[*A*] [no CW on D6v N2 Bb8v]

Copies: B.M. (G. 18852); Bodleian (Percy 27); Oxford, Christ Church; Cambridge, St. John's; Liverpool University; National Library of Wales; Harvard; Huntington; Yale; Folger; New York, Pierpont Morgan Library (W. 2. B); Los Angeles, Clark Library. +

This edition was reissued in 1699 with a fresh title-page, which reads as follows:

[within double rules] THE | WORKS | OF | Mr. JOHN CLEVELAND, | Containing his | *Poems, Orations and Epiſtles*: | ALSO, | The Ruſtick Rampant, | OR, | Rural Anarchy | Affronting | Monarchy, | IN THE | Inſurrection of *WAT. TYLER*; | Collected | Into One Volume, with the LIFE | of the AUTHOR. | [rule] | *LONDON*, | Printed for *O. B.* and are to be Sold by *J. Sprint*, | at the *Bell* in *Little Britain*. 1699.

Copies: B.M. (1076. g. 12); Bodleian (Vet. A3e. 1083); Cambridge, Christ's; London University; Edinburgh University; Wigan Public Library; Liverpool University; Manchester, Chetham's Library; Harvard (*EC. 65. C5993. B687wa); Huntington; Chicago University; Baltimore, Peabody Institute. +

The sheets of the 1687 edition were reissued in 1742, and this is the last issue of Cleveland's poems before the critical editions of the twentieth century. The 1742 issue had a fresh title-page, as follows:

THE | Compleat WORKS | OF | The Late Ingenious and Learned Mr. | *John Cleveland*, in Proſe and Verſe, | Conſiſting of Poems, Letters, and Epi- | ſtles on various Subjects. | To which is Added | An Account of the Inſurrection of *Wat. Tyler* in the Reign | of *King Richard* the Second, Intermixt with ſeveral curi- | ous and Entertaining Relations both Antient and Modern. | [rule] | [ornament] | *LONDON:* | Printed for *J. B[r]own, J. Midwinter J. Clarke,* | M,DCC,XL,II.

Only two copies are known: one in the London Library, the other in the possession of Professor A. Johnston, University College of Wales, Aberystwyth.

J. Cleaveland Revived

29 **CR1** WING C4674

J. Cleaveland Revived: | POEMS, | ORATIONS, | EPISTLES, | And other of his Genuine | Incomparable Pieces, never | before publiſht. | WITH | Some other Exquiſite Remains of | the moſt eminent Wits of both the | Univerſities that were his | Contemporaries. | *Non norunt haec monumenta mori.* | [row of type-orns.] | *LONDON,* | Printed for *Nathaniel Brook,* at the | Angel in Corn-hill. 1659.

Separate title G2 *Jo: Cleveland* | HIS | ORATIONS | AND | EPISTLES, | On Eminent Occaſions, | In Latin. | [rule] | *Engliſh't by* E. W. | [rule] | [triangle of six type-orns.] | [rule] | Printed for *Nath. Brook,* at the Angel | in *Corn-hill.* 1659.

Collation: 8°: A–I[8] K[4] [$4 (—G2 K4) signed], F3 mis-signed E3. 76 leaves, pp. [*16*] 1–82 [83] [84] 85–127 [128] [*8*]. P. 85 centred in hdl. between brackets. Plate, 'Vera Effigies J: Cleaulandi' facing t.p.

HT] A3 [beneath three rows of type-orns.] *To the Diſcerning* | *READER.*
- B1 [beneath three rows of type-orns.] *Upon the* KINGS *return* | *from SCOT-LAND.*
- G3 [beneath three rows of type-orns.] Oratio coram Rege, & Principe *Carolo* | in Collegio *Joannenſi Cantab.* | habita. 1642.
- K1 [beneath a row of type-orns.] Courteous Reader, | *Theſe Books following are ſold by* | Nath. Brook, *at the Angel in* | Cornhill.

RT] A3v–A7v *To the Reader.*
- B1v–G1v *Poems.* [*Poems.* B2 B5 B6 B7 B8 C1 C2 C5 C6 C7 C8 D1 D2 D5 D6 D7 D8 E1 E2 E5 E6 E7 E8 F3 F4 F5 F6 F7 F8]
- G3v–I8 *Orations and Epiſtles.*
- K1v–K4v *Books ſold by* Nath. Brook, | *at the Angel in* Cornhill. [*Books ſold by* Nath. Brook, *&c.* K4v] [no RT on A8 A8v I8v]

A1: Plate. A2: Title (verso blank). A3: To the Discerning Reader. A8: Verses that came too late. (verso blank). B1: Poems. G2: Second Title (verso blank). G3: Orations and Epistles. On I8: *FINIS.* | [rule] | [tail-orn.] | [rule] | I8v: Notice of Errata. K1: Brook's List of Books. On K4v: *FINIS.*

CW] A4 when A7 obliege A7^{v} Verſes B4 *Victuque* B8^{v} *To* C3^{v} VVhich C8^{v} Behold, D6 Plough- [Ploughmen] D8^{v} *In* E4^{v} A face E8^{v} You F1 *On* [*To*] F3^{v} Where [VVhere] F6 Baldneſs [Baldneſſe] F8^{v} But G3^{v} *vixi-* [*viximus*] G4 *An* [An] G7^{v} approach- [approacheth] G8^{v} *cidente* H3 *ſcepiſti)* [*cepiſti)*] H5^{v} Ejuſd. [Ejuſdem] H8^{v} *betha* I2 Goddeſſes, [Goddeſs,] I2^{v} Ejuſ- [Ejuſdem] I3 *mico-* [*micoctus*] I4 *&* *ite-* [*iteratâ*] I6 an [and] K1 *Ex-* [*Excellent*] K3^{v} Like- [Likewiſe] [no CW on A8 G1^{v} I8 I8^{v}]

Copies: B.M. (G. 18854); Bodleian (Douce C. 427); Cambridge, St. John's; Cambridge, Emmanuel; Liverpool University; Harvard; Huntington; Yale; Folger; Los Angeles, Clark Library; Chicago, Newberry Library; New York Public Library. +

30 **CR2** WING C4675

[within double rules] *J. Cleaveland* Revived: | POEMS, | ORATIONS, | EPISTLES, | And other of his Genuine | Incomparable Pieces. | With ſome other Exquiſite Remains of | the moſt eminent Wits of both the Univer- | ſities that were his Contemporaries. | This ſecond Edition, beſides many other | never before publiſht Additions, is enrich- | ed with the Authors *Midſummer-Moon*, | or *Lunacy--rampant*; | Being an Univerſity Character, a ſhort Survey | of ſome of the late Fellows of the Colledges. | Now at laſt publiſht from his Original Copies, | by ſome of his intruſted Friends. | [rule] | *Non norunt haec monumenta mori.* | [rule] | *London*, Printed for *Nathaniel Brooke* at the | *Angel* in Cornhil. 1660.

Separate title I2 *J. CLEAVELAND* | HIS | ORATIONS | AND | EPISTLES, | On Eminent Occaſions, in | Latinc. | *Engliſh't by* E. W. | With an Addition (amongſt others) of an | Univerſity Character, a ſhort Survey of | ſome of the late Renegado Fellows | of the Colledges. | [rule] | *Non norunt haec monumenta wori.* | [rule] | [two rows of five type-orns.] | [rule] | *London*, Printed for *Nath. Brook*, at the Angel | in *Corn-hill.* 1660.

Collation: 8°: A–M^{8} N^{4} [$4 (—G3 N3 N4) signed], H4 mis-signed as H2. 100 leaves, pp. [*10*] 1–7 [8] 9–120 [121] [122] 121–123 126–190. P. 9 centred in hdl. between brackets, p. 121 centred in hdl. Plate, 'Vera Effigies J: Cleaulandi' facing t.p.

HT] A3 [beneath a row of type-orns.] *To the Diſcerning READER.*
A6 [beneath a row of type-orns.] AN ELEGY, | In Memory of | Mr. *John Cleaveland.*

B2 [beneath two rows of type-orns.] UPON THE | KING'S | Return from *Scotland.*

I3 [beneath a row of type-orns.] Oratio coram Rege, & Principe *Carolo* in Col- | legio *Joannenſi Cantab.* habita. 1642.

M7 [beneath a row of type-orns.] Mid-ſummer Moon: | OR, | LUNACY RAMPANT, | Being an Univerſity Character, and a | ſhort Survey of ſome of the late | Fellows of the *Colledges.*

RT] A3^{v}–A5 *To the Reader.*
A6^{v}–I1^{v} *POEMS.*
I3^{v}–M6^{v} *Orations and Epiſtles.* [*Epiſtles.* K3^{v} K8 L7]
M7^{v}–N4^{v} *Mid-ſummer Moon.* [No RT on A5^{v}]

A1: Plate. A2: Title (verso blank). A3: To the Discerning Reader. A5^{v}: The Stationer to the Reader, and On Mr. John Cleaveland. A6: Elegies on Cleveland. B1^{v}: blank. B2: Poems. On I1^{v}: *FINIS.* I2: Second Title (verso blank). I3: Orations and Epistles. M7: Midsummer Moon. N4^{v}: Epitaph on Cleveland, and beneath it *FINIS.* | [rule] | *Books to be ſold by* Nath. Brook *at the Angel in* Cornhil.

CW] A4 neſs A8^{v} Then B1 *Upon* [UPON on B2] B8^{v} And C1 Re- [Rebellis] C8^{v} A *Sol-* [A *Soldier*] D6 Now D8^{v} A ſhep- [A Shepherd] E1^{v} Shall [Shal]E8^{v} Muſt F8^{v} Or G4 So G8^{v} You, H2 With [Where] H8^{v} And I8^{v} Ejuſdem K4^{v} *de-* [*deprimat*] K5 *rolus*! [*rolus!*] K5^{v} there- [therfore] K8^{v} a Chicken, L8^{v} breathing M2 Meto- [Metonimy] M6^{v} Mid- M8^{v} ny N2 have [no CW on A5 I1^{v} I7]

Copies: B.M. (1076. e. 14); Bodleian (Vet. A3f. 679); Oxford, Worcester (LR. 1. 6); Cambridge, St. John's; Victoria and Albert Museum (Forster); University of Glasgow; Harvard; Huntington; Yale; Chicago, Newberry Library; Los Angeles, Clark Library; Boston Public Library. + The Yale copy corrects the signature on H4.

31 CR3 WING C4676

[within a frame of type-orns.] *J. Cleaveland* Revived: | POEMS, | ORATIONS, | EPISTLES, | And other of his Genuine | Incomparable Pieces. | With ſome other Exquiſite Remains of | the moſt eminent Wits of both the Uni- | verſities that were his Contemporaries. | This third Edition, beſides many other | never before publiſht Additions, is en- | riched with the Authors *Midſum-* | *mer-Moon*, or *Lunacy-* | *Rampant.* | Being an Univerſity Character, a ſhort Survey of | ſome of the late Fellows of the Colledges. | Now at laſt publiſht from his Original Co- | pies, by ſome of his intruſted Friends. | [rule] | *Non norunt haec monumenta mori.* | [rule] | *London*, Printed for *Nathaniel Brook*, at the | Angel in *Cornhill.* 1662.

Separate title I2 *J. CLEAVELAND* | HIS | ORATIONS | AND | EPISTLES, | On Eminent Occaſions, in | LATINE. | *Engliſht by* E. W. | With an Addition (amongſt others) of an | Univerſity Character, a ſhort Survey of | ſome of the late Renegado Fellows | of the COLLEDGES. | [rule] | *Non norunt haec Monumenta mori.* | [rule] | [two rows of four type-orns.] | [rule] | *London*, Printed for *Nath. Brooke*, at the Angel | in *Cornhill*. 1662.

Collation: 8°: A–M⁸ N⁴ [$4 (—G3 N3 N4) signed], 100 leaves, pp. [*18*] 1–112 [113] [114] 115–182. P. 1 centred in hdl. between brackets. Plate, 'Vera Effigies J: Cleaulandi' facing t.p.

HT] A3 [beneath a row of type-orns.] *To the Diſcerning* READER.
A6 [beneath a row of type-orns.] AN ELEGY, | In Memory of | Mr. *John Cleaveland.*
B2 [beneath two rows of type-orns.] *J. Cleaveland* Reviv'd. | [rule] | *Upon the KINGS Re-* | *turn from* Scotland.
I3 [beneath a row of type-orns.] Oratio coram Rege, & Principe *Carolo* in Col- | legio *Joannenſi Cantab.* habita. 1642.
M7 [beneath a row of type-orns.] Midſummer Moon: | OR, | LUNACY RAMPANT. | Being an Univerſity Character, and a | ſhort Survey of ſome of the late | Fellows of the Colledges.

RT] A3ᵛ–A5 *To the Reader.*
A6ᵛ–A8ᵛ *Elegies on* J. Cleaveland.
B1 *ELEGIES.*
B2ᵛ–I1ᵛ *POEMS.*
I3ᵛ–M6ᵛ *Orations and Epiſtles.*
M7ᵛ–N4ᵛ *Midſummer Moon.* [*Midſummer* M*oon*. N4 N4ᵛ] [no RT on A5ᵛ]

A1: Plate. A2: Title (verso blank). A3: To the Discerning Reader. A5ᵛ: The Stationer to the Reader, and On Mr. John Cleaveland. A6: Elegies on Cleveland. B1ᵛ: blank. B2: Poems. On I1ᵛ: *FINIS.* I2: Second title (verso blank). I3: Orations and Epistles. M7: Midsummer Moon. N4ᵛ: Epitaph on Cleveland, and beneath it *FINIS.* | [rule] | *Books to be ſold by* Nath. Brook, *at the Angel in* Cornhil.

CW] A4ᵛ of A5ᵛ AN A8ᵛ Then B8 Joy [Joys] B8ᵛ And C1 Re- [Rebellis] C8ᵛ A D5ᵛ Learn- [Learnings] D8ᵛ A E1ᵛ Shall [Shal] E4ᵛ E're [Ere] E8ᵛ Muſt F8ᵛ Or G4ᵛ Thus, G8ᵛ You H2 With [Where] H4ᵛ Where- [Wherefore] H8ᵛ And I1 Windes [Winds] I6ᵛ cle- [clemency] I8ᵛ Ejuſdem K5ᵛ there- [therfore] K8ᵛ a L8 grea- [greater] L8ᵛ breathing M2 Meto- [Metonimy] M6ᵛ Midſummer M8ᵛ ny N2 have [no CW on A5 I1ᵛ I7]

Copies: B.M. (11626. b. 6); Bodleian (Douce C. 428); Cambridge University Library (Syn. 8. 66. 43²); Lambeth Palace Library; Liverpool University;

National Library of Scotland; Harvard; Huntington; Yale; Folger; Chicago, Newberry Library; University of Texas. + Another copy at Yale has title-page and gathering A from CR3 and the remaining gatherings from CR2.

32 CR4 WING C4677

[within a frame of type-orns.] *J. Cleaveland* Revived: | POEMS, | ORATIONS, | EPISTLES, | And other of his Genuine | Incomparable Pieccs. | With ſome other Exquiſite Remains of | moſt eminent Wits of both the Univer- | verſities that were his Contemporaries. | This Fourth Edition, beſides many other ne- | ver before publiſht Additions, is enrich- | ed with the Authors *Midſummer-* | *Moon*, or *Lunacy-Rampant.* | Being an Univerſity Caracter, a ſhort ſurvey of | ſome of the late fellows of the Colledges. | Now at laſt publiſht from his Original Co- | pies by ſome of his intruſted Friends. | [rule] | *Non norunt haec monumenta mori.* | [rule] | *London*, Printed for *Nathaniel Brooks*, at the | *Angell* in *Greſham Colledge*, 1668.

Separate title I2 *J. CLEAVELAND* | HIS | ORATIONS | AND | EPISTLES, | On Eminent Occaſions, in | LATINE. | *Engliſht by* E. W. | With an Addition (amongſt others) of an | Univerſity Character, a ſhort Survey of | ſome of the late Renegado-Fellows | of the *COLLEDGES.* | [rule] | *Non norunt haec Monumenta mori.* | [rule] | [two rows of three type-orns.] | [rule] | *London*, Printed for *Nath. Brooke*, at the Angel | in *Greſham Colledge*. 1667.

Collation: 8°: A–M^8 N^4 [\$4 (—G3 N3 N4) signed], 100 leaves, pp. [*18*] 1–112 [113] [114] 115–182. P. 1 centred in hdl. between brackets. Plate 'Vera Effigies J: Cleaulandi', facing t.p.

HT] A3 [beneath a row of type-orns.] *To the Diſcerning READER.*
A6 [beneath a row of type-orns.] AN ELEGY | In Memory of | Mr. *John Cleaveland.*
B2 [beneath two rows of type-orns.] *J. Cleaveland* Reviv'd. | [rule] | *Vpon the KINGS Re-* | *turn from* Scotland.
I3 [beneath a row of type-orns.] Oratio coram Rege, & Principe *Carolo* in Col- | legio *Joannenſi Cantab.* habita. 1642.
M7 [beneath a row of type-orns.] Midſummer Moon. | OR, | LVNACY RAMPANT. | Being an Vniverſitie Character, and | a ſhort Survey of ſome of the late | Fellows of the Colledges.

RT] A3^v–A5 *To the Reader.* [*Reader* A4^v]
A6^v–A8^v *Elegies on* J. Cleaveland.
B1 *ELEGIES.*

B2^{v}–I1^{v} *POEMS.* [*POEMS.* B2^{v} C2^{v} D2^{v} E1^{v} F2^{v} G2^{v} H2^{v}; *POEMS.* B4 B5 B6 B7 C4 C5 C6 C7 D4 D5 D6 D7 E5 E6 E8 F6 G6 H6; *POEMS.* B8^{v} C2 C8^{v} D2 D8^{v} E1 E7^{v} F2 F8^{v} G2 G8^{v} H2 H8^{v}; *POEMS.* C1^{v} D1^{v} E2^{v} F1^{v} G1^{v} H1^{v} I1^{v}; *POEMS.* E3 F4 G4 H4]

I3^{v}–M6^{v} *Orations and Epiſtles.* [*Epistles.* I4^{v} I6 I7^{v} K1^{v} K2^{v} L4^{v} L7^{v} M2^{v} M5^{v}; *Epiſtles.* I8 K6 K7^{v} L2 L6 L8 M2 M4]

M7^{v}–N4^{v} *Midſummer Moon.* [*Moon.* M8^{v} N1^{v} N2; *Moon-* N2^{v}; *Midſummer* N3^{v}] [no RT on A5^{v}]

A1: Plate. A2: Title (verso blank). A3: To the Discerning Reader. A5^{v}: The Stationer to the Reader, and On Mr. John Cleaveland. A6: Elegies on Cleveland. B1^{v}: blank. B2: Poems. On I1^{v}: *FINIS.* I2: Second title (verso blank). I3: Orations and Epistles. M7 Midsummer Moon. N4^{v}: Epitaph on Cleveland, and beneath it *FINIS.* | [rule] | *Books to be ſold by* Nath. Brook, *at the Angel in* Greſham- | Colledge.

CW] A3^{v} *friends* A5^{v} AN B3 *T*hen [Then] B8 Joy [Joys] B8^{v} And C8^{v} *A* [A] D4 '*T*would ['Twould] D8^{v} A E1 ſuch [Such] E1^{v} Shall [Shal] E2 '*T*is ['Tis] E6 *T*hoſe [Thoſe] E8^{v} Muſt F6 *T*his [This] F7 *Occanum-* [*Oceanumque*] F8^{v} Or G3 VVith [With] G6 Withou [Without] G7^{v} 7. So [7. Sobriety] G8^{v} You H2 With [Where] H4^{v} Where- [Wherefore] H8^{v} And I1 Windes [Winds] I3^{v} *Vivas,* [*Vivas*] I8^{v} Ejuſdem K5^{v} there- [therefore] L8 grea- [greater] L8^{v} breathing M2 Meto- [Metonimy] M6^{v} Midſummer M8^{v} ny N2 have [no CW on A5 B1 I1^{v} I7 K8^{v}]

Copies: B.M. (1163. a. 28); Bodleian (Radcliffe f. 84); Oxford, Balliol; Cambridge, St.John's; Liverpool University; Harvard; Huntington; Folger; Chicago University; New York Public Library; Los Angeles, Clark Library; Berlin, Deutsche Staatsbibliothek. +

APPENDIX

CONTENTS OF THE EDITIONS

	D1	D1A	D2	D2A	D3	D4	D5	D6	P1	P1A	P2	P3	P4	P5	P6	P7	P8	P9	P10	P11	P12	P13	P14	P15	P16	P17	CV	W	CR1	CR2	CR3	CR4
Upon an Hermophrodite	×	×	×	×	×	×	×	×	×	×	×	×	×	×	×	×	×	×	×	×	×	×	×	×	×	×	×	×				
The Authors Hermophrodite	×	×	×	×	×	×	×	×	×	×	×	×	×	×	×	×	×	×	×	×	×	×	×	×	×	×	×	×				
Upon Phillis	×	×	×	×	×	×	×	×	×	×	×	×	×	×	×	×	×	×	×	×	×	×	×	×	×	×	×	×				
Upon a Miser	×	×	×	×	×	×	×	×	×	×	×	×	×	×	×	×	×	×	×	×	×	×	×	×	×	×	×	×				
Young Man to an Old Woman	×	×	×	×	×	×	×	×	×	×	×	×	×	×	×	×	×	×	×	×	×	×	×	×	×	×	×	×				
To Mrs. K. T.	×	×	×	×	×	×	×	×	×	×	×	×	×	×	×	×	×	×	×	×	×	×	×	×	×	×	×	×				
A Faire Nimph	×	×	×	×	×	×	×	×	×	×	×	×	×	×	×	×	×	×	×	×	×	×	×	×	×	×	×	×				
Dialogue between Two Zealots	×	×	×	×	×	×	×	×	×	×	×	×	×	×	×	×	×	×	×	×	×	×	×	×	×	×	×	×				
Smectymnuus	×	×	×	×	×	×	×	×	×	×	×	×	×	×	×	×	×	×	×	×	×	×	×	×	×	×	×	×				
The Mixt Assembly	×	×	×	×	×	×	×	×	×	×	×	×	×	×	×	×	×	×	×	×	×	×	×	×	×	×	×	×				
The Kings Disguise	×	×	×	×	×	×	×	×	×	×	×	×	×	×	×	×	×	×	×	×	×	×	×	×	×	×	×	×				
The Rebell Scot	×	×	×	×	×	×	×	×	×	×	×	×	×	×	×	×	×	×	×	×	×	×	×	×	×	×	×	×		×	×	×
To P. Rupert	×	×	×	×	×	×	×	×	×	×	×	×	×	×	×	×	×	×	×	×	×	×	×	×	×	×	×	×				
Epitaph on Strafford	×	×	×	×	×	×	×	×	×	×	×	×	×	×	×	×	×	×	×	×	×	×	×	×	×	×		×				
Epitaphium Thomae	×	×	×	×	×	×	×	×	×	×	×	×	×	×	×	×	×	×	×	×	×	×	×	×	×	×		×				
On the Archbishop of Canterbury	×	×	×	×	×	×	×	×	×	×	×	×	×	×	×	×	×	×	×	×	×	×	×	×	×	×	×	×				
On I. W. Archbishop of York	×	×	×	×	×	×	×	×	×	×	×	×	×	×	×	×	×	×	×	×	×	×	×	×	×	×		×				
Marke Anthony		×		×		×	×	×	×	×	×	×	×	×	×	×	×	×	×	×	×	×	×	×	×	×	×	×				
Mock Song to Marke Anthony		×		×		×	×	×	×	×	×	×	×	×	×	×	×	×	×	×	×	×	×	×	×	×	×	×				
Britanicus his Blessing				×																												
Britanicus his Welcome				×																												

	D1	D1A	D2	D2A	D3	D4	D5	D6	P1	P1A	P2	P3	P4	P5	P6	P7	P8	P9	P10	P11	P12	P13	P14	P15	P16	P17	CV	W	CR1	CR2	CR3	CR4
Square Cap							×	×	×	×	×	×	×	×	×	×	×	×	×	×	×	×	×	×	×	×	×	×				
On the Death of Mr. King							×	×	×	×	×	×	×	×	×	×	×	×	×	×	×	×	×	×	×	×	×	×				
The Scots Apostasy							×	×	×	×	×	×	×	×	×	×	×	×	×	×	×	×	×	×	×	×		×				
A New Litany								×																								
The Senses Festivall									×	×	×	×	×	×	×	×	×	×	×	×	×	×	×	×	×	×	×	×				
Hecatomb to his Mistress									×	×	×	×	×	×	×	×	×	×	×	×	×	×	×	×	×	×	×	×				
Upon Sir Thomas Martin									×	×	×	×	×	×	×	×	×	×	×	×	×	×	×	×	×	×	×	×				
Second poem on King									×	×	×	×	×	×	×	×	×	×	×	×	×	×	×	×	×	×						
Hue & Cry after Sir John Presbyter										×	×	×	×	×	×	×	×	×	×	×	×	×	×	×	×	×	×	×				
The Antiplatonick										×	×	×	×	×	×	×	×	×	×	×	×	×	×	×	×	×	×	×				
How the Commencement grows new											×	×	×	×	×	×	×	×	×	×	×	×	×	×	×	×	×	×				
Fuscara											×	×	×	×	×	×	×	×	×	×	×	×	×	×	×	×	×	×				
Elegy on Chaderton											×	×	×	×	×	×	×	×	×	×	×	×	×	×	×	×		×				
Maries Spikenard											×	×	×	×	×	×	×	×	×	×	×	×	×	×	×	×		×				
To the Hectors														×	×	×	×	×	×	×	×	×	×	×	×	×		×				
To Julia															×	×	×	×	×	×	×	×	×	×	×	×	×	×				
Chronostichon															×	×	×	×	×	×	×	×	×	×	×	×		×				
Elegy on King Charles															×	×	×	×	×	×	×	×	×	×	×	×		×				
Elegy on the Best of Men															×	×	×	×	×	×	×	×	×	×	×	×		×				
Montrose's Elegy on Charles															×	×	×	×	×	×	×	×	×	×	×	×		×				
On a Scratch on a Ladies Arm																				×	×											
Parting with a Friend on the Way																				×	×											
On a Gentlewoman (Oft shall you see)																				×	×											
On Princess Elizabeth																				×	×						×	×				
Humane Inconstancie																				×	×											
Englands Jubile																				×	×											

The Four-Legg'd Elder	×							
'Some Christian People'	×							
A Sigh		×	×	×	×	×		×
The Publick Faith		×	×	×	×	×		×
A Lenten Litany		×	×	×	×	×		×
Hue & Cry after the Reformation		×	×	×	×	×		×
A Committee		×	×	×	×	×		×
On the Memory of Alderman Hoyle		×	×	×	×	×		×
Platonique Love		×	×	×	×	×		×
Christmas Day		×	×	×	×	×		×
Piae Memoriae		×	×	×	×	×		×
Obsequies (If by the fall)		×	×	×	×	×		×
On the Death of his Royal Majesty		×	×	×	×	×		×
An Epitaph (Stay Passenger)		×	×	×	×	×		×
A Survey of the World		×	×	×	×	×		×
An Old Man Courting a Young Girl		×	×	×	×	×		×
Epitaph on his Deceased Friend		×	×	×	×	×		×
Mount Ida		×	×	×	×	×		×
Upon a Flye		×	×	×	×	×		×
Obsequies (What ? The whole world)		×	×	×	×	×		×
The London Lady		×	×	×	×	×		×
The Times		×	×	×	×	×		×
The Model of the New Religion		×	×	×	×	×		×
On Britanicus his leap		×	×	×	×	×		×
Content		×	×	×	×	×		×
May Day		×	×	×	×	×		×

	D1	D1A	D2	D2A	D3	D4	D5	D6	P1	P1A	P2	P3	P4	P5	P6	P7	P8	P9	P10	P11	P12	P13	P14	P15	P16	P17	CV	W	CR1	CR2	CR3	CR4
Epigram to Doulus																						×	×	×	×	×		×				
Epigram on the people of England																						×	×	×	×	×		×				
Another on the same																						×	×	×	×	×		×				
Sing-Song on Clarinda's Wedding																						×	×	×	×	×		×				
The Myrtle Grove																						×	×	×	×	×		×				
To my honour'd friend Mr. T. C.																						×	×	×	×	×		×				
The Engagement Stated																						×	×	×	×	×		×				
Praelegenda to The Wife Hater																						×	×	×	×	×		×				
Vituperium Uxoris																						×	×	×	×	×		×				
Elegy on Cleveland (Prime Wits)																						×	×	×	×	×		×				
Upon the pittiful Elegy																						×	×	×	×	×		×				
The Kings Return																											×	×	×	×	×	×
On a talkative woman																												×	×	×	×	×
Rebellis Scotus																											×	×	×	×	×	×
On an Ugly Woman																												×	×	×	×	×
To the King recovered from sickness																												×	×	×	×	×
On a little Gentleman																												×	×	×	×	×
On the birth of the Duke of York																												×	×	×	×	×
On Parsons the Great Porter																												×	×	×	×	×
To the Queen (That children are)																												×	×	×	×	×
To Cloris, a Rapture																												×	×	×	×	×
Elegy on Jonson (As when the)																												×	×	×	×	×
Epitaph (Stay Gentle Reader)																												×	×	×	×	×
Upon Wood of Kent																												×	×	×	×	×
On Christ-church windows																												×	×	×	×	×
Entertainment at Cotswold																													×			

To the Queen (Whom Tumults)	×	×	×	×	×
Elegy on Jonson (Poet of Princes)	×	×	×	×	×
On Ben Jonson (Who first reform'd)	×	×	×	×	×
To his Mistresse (Come dearest Julia)	×	×	×	×	×
In Nuptias Principis Auranchii	×	×	×	×	×
On the Prince of Orange's Wedding	×	×	×	×	×
Another on the same (Tis vain to)	×	×	×	×	×
Epitaph on Jonson (The Muses)	×	×	×	×	×
On one deprived of his testicles	×	×	×	×	×
To his Mistresse (What mystery is)	×	×	×	×	×
The Puritan	×	×	×	×	×
The Flight	×	×	×	×	×
To a Lady (Could we judge here)	×	×	×	×	×
To the King (The Prince hath now)	×	×	×	×	×
To the Queen (After the Princes)	×	×	×	×	×
On one that preach't in a cloak	×	×	×	×	×
On the May Pole	×	×	×	×	×
To the Queen (If Poets could be)	×	×	×	×	×
On the Tom of Christ-Church	×	×	×	×	×
On a burning glass	×	×	×	×	×
On Sheriff Sandbourn	×	×	×	×	×
Not to travel	×	×	×	×	×
Elegy (Soon as a verse)	×		×	×	×
Elegy (Grief the Souls Sables)	×		×	×	×
Elegy (Poor Dablers all bemir'd)	×		×	×	×
Elegy (He whom the Muses)	×		×	×	×

	D1	D1A	D2	D2A	D3	D4	D5	D6	P1	P1A	P2	P3	P4	P5	P6	P7	P8	P9	P10	P11	P12	P13	P14	P15	P16	P17	CV	W	CR1	CR2	CR3	CR4
News from Newcastle																												×		×	×	×
Inundation of River Trent																												×		×	×	×
For Sleep																												×		×	×	×
Against Sleep																												×		×	×	×
On his going by water																												×		×	×	×
On coming into a chamber																												×		×	×	×
Against Ale																												×		×	×	×
The Old Gill																												×		×	×	×
A Sad Suit																												×		×	×	×
The Poor Cavalier																												×		×	×	×
The Ruins of St. Pauls																												×		×	×	×
Relation of a Quaker																												×		×	×	×
Scots Apostasy (Part 2)																												×		×	×	×
Antiplatonick (Fond love what dost)																												×		×	×	×
Definition of a Protector																												×		×	×	×
On the Invention of Flying																												×		×	×	×
The Coachman of St. James'es																												×		×	×	×
On Black Eyes																												×		×	×	×
A Song of Sack																												×		×	×	×
A Time Sonnet																												×		×	×	×
The Parliament																												×		×	×	×
The Schismatick																												×		×	×	×
A Zealous Discourse																												×		×	×	×
On O. P. Sick																												×		×	×	×
An Answer to the Storm																												×		×	×	×
Epitaph (Who with true fire)																														×	×	×

Umbra diu Elisii lacrymabilis	×	×
Hail venerable Reliques	×	×
Quid video ? video et laetor	×	×
Qui metricis nollet pedibus	×	×
Clieveland again his sacred head	×	×
The General Eclipse	×	×
Epitaphium Thomae Spell	×	×

PRINTED IN GREAT BRITAIN
AT THE UNIVERSITY PRESS, OXFORD
BY VIVIAN RIDLER
PRINTER TO THE UNIVERSITY